The World's Worst Disasters Did Not All Lead to Gloom!

Now the Ripley's researchers have dug into history to find the facts of all the great disasters from the Chicago fire to the Johnstown flood. But they're not all without humor— what about the man who sold earthquake pills to the people of London so they wouldn't be hurt by a quake?

The stories are amazing, astonishing, astounding and true—and you'd better believe it!

If you cannot find your favorite **Believe It or Not!** POCKET BOOK at your local newsstand, please write to the nearest Ripley's "Believe It or Not!" museum:

19 San Marco Avenue, St. Augustine, Florida 32084

901 North Ocean Blvd., Myrtle Beach, South Carolina 29577

175 Jefferson Street, San Francisco, California 94133

145 East Elkhorn Avenue, Estes Park, Colorado 80517

Rebel Corners, Gatlinburg, Tennessee 37738

1500 North Wells Street, Chicago, Illinois 60610

4960 Clifton Hill, Niagara Falls, Canada L2G 3N5

Boardwalk and Wicomico, Ocean City, Maryland 21842

Ripley's
Believe It or Not!
GREAT
DISASTERS

PUBLISHED BY POCKET BOOKS NEW YORK

Another *Original* publication of POCKET BOOKS

POCKET BOOKS, a Simon & Schuster division of
GULF & WESTERN CORPORATION
1230 Avenue of the Americas, New York, N.Y. 10020

ISBN: 0-671-82068-0

First Pocket Books printing August, 1979

10 9 8 7 6 5 4 3 2 1

Contents

Published by POCKET BOOKS

Ripley's
Believe It or Not!®
GREAT
DISASTERS

. . . We have all heard of cities of South America built upon the side of fiery mountains, and how, even in this tremendous neighborhood, the inhabitants are not a jot more impressed by the solemnity of mortal conditions than if they were delving gardens in the greenest corner of England. There are serenades and suppers and much gallantry among the myrtles overhead; and meanwhile the foundation shudders underfoot, the bowels of the mountain growl, and at any moment living ruin may leap sky-high into the moonlight, and tumble man and his merry-making in the dust. . . ."

—*Robert Louis Stevenson*

Introduction

The first recorded disaster to befall Mankind was also undoubtedly the worst: Eve offered an apple and Adam ate. Man was forever banished from the Garden of Eden and condemned to live in a world where chill winds blew, where the ground could open beneath his feet, where rampaging floods or torrents of boiling lava might at any moment reduce his home to a mound of rubble or smoldering ash. A world where insect hordes devoured his crops, where rats and fleas carried deadly infections, where storms of unimaginable fury leveled in an instant what had taken him years to build. It was at best a harsh and uncertain world in which Man was fated to struggle for survival.

But what has proved even more astonishing than Man's ability to *survive* these dreadful calamities has been his strength in *overcoming* them, the courage and resilience displayed by people all over the world who have withstood the shock of disaster and gone on to rebuild their cities, their lives, their hopes. After being crushed by a massive tsunami (tidal wave) in 1900, the entire city of Galveston, Texas, was raised seventeen feet and built again! Rome, London, Chicago—they're all thriving cities today, but all were once ravaged by uncontrollable

FOUNDING FATHER
ACUTELY AWARE OF THE NEED FOR PROTECTION FROM THE EFFECTS OF NATURAL AND MAN-MADE DISASTERS, BENJAMIN FRANKLIN FOUNDED THE **FIRST** AMERICAN INSURANCE COMPANY **AND** THE FIRST VOLUNTEER FIRE BRIGADE!

fires. Managua, Nicaragua, has a fantastic history all its own—three times destroyed by earthquakes, once by floodwaters, devastated by the explosion of an arsenal in 1902, and again, ten years later, ruined in a violent civil war.

From time immemorial, the stoical Chinese have endured the terrible floods of the Yellow River. For centuries, the industrious Dutch have repaired and rebuilt the dikes that protect their country from frequent invasions by the cold North Sea. In all countries, on every continent, men and women have risen above sudden disaster and tragic accident, to reaffirm our human fortitude. Even as the "unsinkable" *Titanic* slipped beneath the freezing ocean waters, the band bravely stayed on deck, playing the hymn "Autumn" to stem the panic. It is to that spirit and resolve that this book, *Great Disasters,* is dedicated.

RIPLEY INTERNATIONAL LTD.
Toronto, Canada

Volcanoes

Sacrifice to La Soufrière

The Carib Indians of the West Indies, for whom the Caribbean Sea was named, believed that they would one day be sacrificed to the fire god they revered. It was a prophecy that would be tragically fulfilled.

Most of the tribe lived on the island of St. Vincent, at the base of the volcano called La Soufrière (the Sulphur Pit). In 1812, after a year of earthquake tremors, the volcano began to throw out ashes and stones. A little boy, herding cattle on the mountain slopes, was hit by bits of the falling debris and thought they had been thrown by other boys hiding behind nearby rocks. He hurled some stones back at what he supposed to be their hiding places. Only afterwards did he happen to look up at the sky where he saw a terrifying cloud of black smoke and cinders billowing up from the crater of La Soufrière. He ran for his life.

For three days, the rumbling continued, and then a torrent of lava spilled from the crater and ran down to the sea. Under thousands of square miles of land there were strange thundering sounds so violent that in some distant cities the people prepared for an armed attack. They mistook the subterranean roar for the sound of cannons firing!

For nearly a hundred years after this outbreak, the volcano was quiet. But in early May, 1902, at the same time Mt. Pelée erupted on Martinique, La Soufrière awoke again, this time more destructively, pouring six streams of molten lava down its sides. Hundreds of people were trapped between the deadly streams and many who escaped were struck by wild lightning bolts. The very foundation of the volcano shook and a cloud of black smoke rose eight miles above the glowing crater.

Days later when the eruption ended all the island's crops and vegetation had been burned away. Homes had utterly disappeared and the riverbeds ran with slowly cooling lava. Two thousand people were dead, including all but a few survivors of the Carib tribe. The fire god they had worshiped for so long had finally claimed his promised sacrifice.

The lava flows from Mount Etna's explosion in 1669 were slowly descending upon the Sicilian town of Catania. The men of the town worked feverishly to divert the channel of the molten river—and succeeded!—until the people of a nearby town now in the lava's path attacked them and forced them to stop.

The lava once again flowed inexorably toward Catania, where it surmounted a protective wall *60 feet high* and consumed most of the town!

The mighty explosion of Mount Skaptar in 1783 nearly brought an end to Iceland. The clouds of ash emitted by the eruption were so vast that they ruined crops as far away as Norway and Scotland. In Iceland itself a bluish haze settled over the coun-

REPRIEVED BY A VOLCANO!

MT. PELEE'S FIERY ERUPTION IN 1902 KILLED ALL 30,000 INHABITANTS OF ST. PIERRE -- EXCEPT ONE, RAOUL SARTERET -- A CONVICTED MURDERER WHO WITNESSED THE DEBACLE FROM HIS DUNGEON CELL! BLINDED BY VOLCANIC GASES, SARTERET WAS PARDONED -- AND WENT ON TO BECOME *A RESPECTED MISSIONARY!*

HOME OF THE ANGRY GODS!

EVERY HUNDRED YEARS THE BALINESE WORSHIPPED THEIR VOLCANO GOD, AGUNG, IN A TEMPLE ON THE MOUNTAIN'S SLOPE. DURING THE 1963 CENTENNIAL WHILE THOUSANDS PAID HOMAGE TO THEIR GODS, THE VOLCANO EXPLODED, EMITTING A DEADLY GAS *WHICH KILLED EVERY LIVING CREATURE IN A RADIUS OF TEN MILES!*

18

try all summer, grass and crops perished, and in turn livestock and people. Before this "Haze Famine" had lifted, Iceland had lost 230,000 head of cattle, and one-fifth of its human inhabitants!

The Destruction of Pompeii

The morning of August 24th, 79 A.D., broke in an ominous fashion. Above long dormant Mount Vesuvius, there rose a cloud of smoke that gradually grew and spread across the sky. As the hours passed, the volcano began to emit hot ashes and chunks of pumice, and the people in the nearby towns grew alarmed. Some fled, but others, for a variety of reasons, chose to stay—to protect their possessions, to loot what others had left behind, or simply because they couldn't imagine the horror that was about to unfold.

That night, the ash-fall continued and sulfurous vapors made the air increasingly difficult to breathe. The ground trembled. By morning, the sky was dark with the dust and ash, and the citizens of Pompeii, so close to the erupting volcano, made for the safety of the open fields. Suddenly, a dense black cloud engulfed the entire area making it impossible for families to find each other or for anyone to find refuge. For hours, the ash filled the air and people had to shake it off their bodies or be buried alive. When the sky finally began to lighten and the air to clear, the survivors of Vesuvius' mighty explosion looked around to see miles of countryside covered with a thick mantle of gray ash. Vesuvius itself had been reduced from a huge, smooth cone to a sawed-off stump.

WHEN CRIME STOOD STILL!

AMONG THE MANY CITIZENS OF POMPEII PETRIFIED FOREVER IN THE VOLCANIC MUD SPEWING FROM MT. VESUVIUS, WAS A MAN DEFENDING HIS RICHES WITH A SWORD. AROUND HIS STILL-STANDING FIGURE LAY THE PETRIFIED BODIES OF *FIVE WOULD-BE THIEVES!*

But the greatest horrors of the eruption befell those who remained in the town. Most had choked to death on the sulfurous gases that blew into the streets. Others died when the roofs of their houses collapsed under the weight of the falling ash. Indeed, the town was buried so deep in the volcanic debris that only the very tops of some of the tallest buildings could be seen. The survivors of Pompeii—financially ruined, broken in spirit—abandoned what little that was left of the town.

For centuries, Pompeii was lost. It wasn't until the eighteenth century that the city was identified and excavation began. At that time, in one of history's grimmest and most amazing footnotes, the bodies of many who perished in the cataclysmic eruption were discovered, preserved as nearly-perfect fossils! The dense ashfall which smothered them had been followed by a heavy rain; a kind of cement had formed around the bodies of the victims, and nineteenth-century archaeologists were able to extract three-dimensional casts. The detail preserved on some of these figures is astounding, complete down to the very expression on the face. Many are clutching their throats, suffocating on the deadly gases in the air. Others are attempting to make off with jewelry or gold. Excavators even found a dog which had been buried alive while chained to a post!

Their petrified agonies will attest forever to the terrible fate of Pompeii.

When mighty Vesuvius began to erupt again in 1906, the people of San Giuseppe abandoned their homes and ran to take refuge in the village church.

It was there, while they prayed for deliverance, that the roof gave way under the enormous weight of the volcanic ash and crashed down on the congregation!

Ironically, the villagers might have saved themselves—and their houses—simply by staying home and shovelling the ash off their roofs before it had a chance to accumulate.

Birth of a Volcano

Everyday, a Mexican-Indian farmer named Dionisio Pulido went out to his fields to tend his crops. But one morning he was surprised to find the earth warm and trembling beneath his feet. For three weeks his cornfield shook. One day he discovered a tiny spout of steam shooting up from a hole in the ground. The hole widened rapidly; it was thirty feet across in just a matter of hours, and by nightfall it was spitting burning hot cinders into the air. The morning sun revealed a cone one hundred twenty feet high!

Two nearby towns, Paricutin and San Juan, were obliterated by the lava and ash. Within two years of its birth, the newly-christened Paricutin volcano had gone from a steam-hole only a few inches wide to a mighty mountain standing fifteen hundred feet!

The Princess and the Planes

On two separate occasions, the city of Hilo has barely escaped destruction from lava flows—once, according to the native Hawaiians, through the intervention of a beautiful princess, and once with the help of United States Navy bombers!

When the mighty volcano Mauna Loa erupted in 1880, a veritable ocean of molten lava crept down the mountainside and slowly moved toward Hilo. For a period of six months, the lava flowed, spreading over an area of land larger than Rhode Island and to a depth of several feet, but within a half-mile of the city itself the lava miraculously halted! The Hawaiians claimed that the city had been spared because the Princess Kamahamena had thrown a lock of her beautiful hair into the fiery mass in order to placate the raging volcano.

But the volcano was only temporarily mollified. In 1935, Mauna Loa erupted again, and again a torrent of lava relentlessly traveled toward Hilo at a rate of well over a mile a day. This time, the Hawaiians relied on the U.S. Navy. Bombers dropped 6,000 pounds of bombs on the lava flow, changing its direction and once again saving the city of Hilo from destruction.

Valley of Ten Thousand Smokes

In the month of June 1912, Mt. Katmai, a volcano in southwest Alaska, exploded with terrific force, throwing up a blanket of dust and ash that darkened the sky for nearly three days. On an island one hundred miles away, the falling ashes made a layer *one foot deep,* and some areas of Canada suffered through a rain of sulfuric acid that rotted people's clothing!

But it wasn't until four years later that scientists

IN 126 B.C. LAVA FLOWS FROM MOUNT ETNA BOILED THE FISH IN THE IONIAN SEA AND THREW THEM ON SHORE, WHERE MANY RESIDENTS ATE SO MANY, SO FAST, THAT THEY BECAME ILL AND DIED!

decided to investigate the after-effects of the eruption. To their amazement, they discovered a valley, miles away from Mt. Katmai, spewing out steam and gas through countless holes in the ground! Appropriately enough, they named the place The Valley of Ten Thousand Smokes, and in 1918 President Woodrow Wilson declared it a national monument.

Tin Can Island

Niuafou, a South Pacific island which is in fact nothing more than the rim of the crater of a huge sub-marine volcano, was once known as Tin Can Island because mail from the outside world was delivered there inside tin cans! But that's not all that's unusual about Niuafou.

A Polynesian tribe called the Tongans have lived for centuries *inside* the crater of the volcano, which erupted as recently as 1943!

Niuafou is also the site of a village called Ahua, which had reportedly been established by people who refused to submit to the strict marriage codes and high taxes imposed upon them in their native village. They moved to the other end of the island, where their headman asked that the gods destroy his people sooner than let them pay the exorbitant taxes. The gods were surprisingly cooperative. On the night of June 24, 1853, a fissure opened right under the headman's hut and molten lava shot upwards out of it. The crack ran straight through Ahua and nearly 70 of the revolutionaries were engulfed by the lava and flames!

THE LOUDEST EXPLOSION IN HISTORY!

THE FIERY EXPLOSION OF KRAKATOA WAS HEARD IN SUCH FARAWAY PLACES AS TEXAS AND CAUSED TIDAL WAVES **120 FEET HIGH THAT KILLED THOUSANDS!**

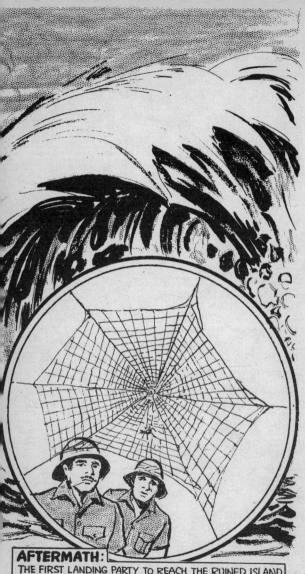

AFTERMATH:
THE FIRST LANDING PARTY TO REACH THE RUINED ISLAND
FOUND NOTHING ALIVE -- *EXCEPT ONE RED SPIDER
SPINNING ITS WEB* !

SENT TO INVESTIGATE AN UNDERWATER VOLCANO, THE JAPANESE RESEARCH SHIP **KAIYO-MARU** WAS SUDDENLY BLOWN TO SMITHEREENS BY A MIGHTY ERUPTION <u>BENEATH THE SEA</u>!

Dynamite Discovery

When the Mexican workers began to dynamite the prehistoric lava flows in order to remove basalt for highway construction, they had no idea what they would find buried underneath! Human skeletons, broken bits of handmade pottery, small figures made of clay. Archaeologists and paleontologists rushed to the spot and after investigating the artifacts determined that one or more Indian villages had been overwhelmed by massive streams of red-hot lava, somewhere between three and ten thousand years ago! Today, tunnels have been dug under the thick layers of lava, and visitors can view the remains of what may well have been our continent's oldest culture!

Even in the Bible, there are records of volcanic activity. It's thought, for example, that the cities of Sodom and Gomorrah were destroyed by a violent eruption.

'Then the Lord rained upon Sodom and Gomorrah brimstone and fire from the Lord out of heaven.
'And He overthrew those cities and all the plain, and all the inhabitants of the cities and that which grew upon the ground. But Lot's wife looked back from behind him, and she became a pillar of salt.'

It sounds as if Lot's wife didn't escape fast enough from the mounting ashes and burning cinders spewed out of the volcano. Her fate was probably the same as that of many Pompeiians, trapped years later by Vesuvius' fury.

Although the exact sites of Sodom and Gomorrah have never been found, they're generally considered to have been close to the Red Sea, a theory borne out by the bitumen found there—a positive indicator of volcanic activity in the past.

Descent into the Inferno

Mihara Yama is an active volcano on the island of Oshima. The Japanese call it "God's Fire Stove" and believe that anyone who commits suicide by leaping into its crater will find eternal peace. In 1933 alone, over two hundred people perished by jumping into the fiery crater.

In 1934, a prominent Japanese newspaper set out to explore this myth by lowering two of its staff members into the volcano. A steel carriage with glass windows was constructed, and the two men dressed in asbestos suits and gas masks stepped inside. The carriage was then swung out over the crater by an enormous crane and lowered inside by pulleys. After descending about five hundred feet, the air cleared enough for the men to observe boiling lava and mud seeping out of cracks in the walls. Huge explosions from below caused the carriage to tremble. As the descent continued, they began to see the bodies of the many suicides. Deep in the crater they spotted two bodies together, waitresses wearing their kimonos from work, sprawled on a small outcropping of rock.

Well over a thousand feet down, the newspaper men signalled the pulley operators to bring them up. The explosions from the lava bed were so violent that they feared the car would be smashed to pieces against the walls of the crater.

When they emerged triumphantly from "God's Fire Stove," they had not only undercut a superstitious belief, but broken a world record for descent into the earth. They had gone over four hundred feet deeper than the seismologist A. Kerner, who had descended into the Stromboli volcano.

2

Earthquakes

The Destruction of Lisbon

On the morning of November 1, 1755, many of Lisbon's citizens were crowded into the city's churches to observe All Hallows Day. As they knelt in prayer in Portugal's capital, the ground beneath them suddenly trembled and lurched. The churches, and countless other buildings, crumbled, spilling tons of heavy masonry and timber down on the people inside. This first shock was followed by two others. Tens of thousands lay crushed beneath the rubble of the city. Others fled to the waterfront to escape the falling buildings. As they huddled in terror on the quays, watching the smoldering ruins of their homes, they were suddenly overwhelmed by gigantic waves that the earthquake had created. They were swept out to sea, as were thousands more when the tsunami hit the coast of Morocco. Its effects were felt over an area covering a million square miles! Chandeliers were set swinging 1400 miles away, and the rocking of the water in the ports of Amsterdam, Rotterdam and Dartmouth was so violent that ships were torn loose from their moorings! The death toll from the Lisbon earthquake—one of the most violent in recorded history—would finally rise to 60,000!

THE **DESTRUCTION** OF THE FOURTH WONDER OF THE WORLD!

IN 365 A.D. A CATASTROPHIC EARTHQUAKE TOPPLED THE 600-FOOT-HIGH LIGHTHOUSE IN ALEXANDRIA, EGYPT... WHOSE BEACON WAS VISIBLE AT A DISTANCE OF *30 MILES!* ITS FOUNDATION ALONE REMAINED *FOR THE NEXT 5 CENTURIES!*

Record Breakers

Seismographs may be our best way of measuring earthquakes—but they're not infallible! An earthquake in Turkey in 1939 damaged instruments in Faenza, Italy, and broke a seismograph as far away as London!

A Los Angeles quake in 1971 knocked out the seismograph in Pasadena, home of Dr. Charles Richter, inventor of the Richter Scale for measuring earthquake intensity!

The Great San Francisco Earthquake

San Francisco slept quietly in the early morning hours of April 19th, 1906, but deep beneath the city the earth was being rent apart. The great San Andreas Fault was stirring and just before the sun rose on Wednesday morning the city suddenly shook with a violent spasm. People were thrown from their beds, hotels crumbled and fissures six feet wide opened in the streets! As horrified San Franciscans spilled out of their homes, the ground suddenly shook again. More buildings toppled, gas and water mains burst apart and a gigantic wave smashed into the waterfront docks!

On Market Street, San Francisco's main thoroughfare, a frenzied crowd of half-dressed people swarmed through the wreckage and falling debris.

A horse and cart went speeding down an avenue, then suddenly plunged into a huge crack in the pavement. The panic-stricken crowd that followed

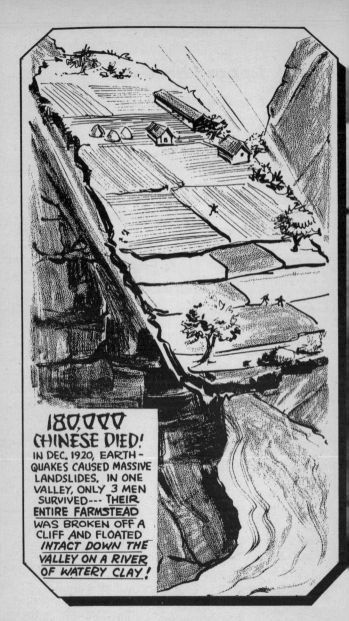

180,000 CHINESE DIED! IN DEC. 1920, EARTH-QUAKES CAUSED MASSIVE LANDSLIDES. IN ONE VALLEY, ONLY 3 MEN SURVIVED--- THEIR ENTIRE FARMSTEAD WAS BROKEN OFF A CLIFF AND FLOATED *INTACT DOWN THE VALLEY ON A RIVER OF WATERY CLAY!*

behind it unwittingly pushed dozens of helpless people into the crevice, too!

At the waterfront pandemonium reigned! People attempting to escape the crumbling city leaped onto any boat in the harbor, but the rough seas proved too much for the overcrowded craft and dozens of boats capsized.

But the worst effects of the quake were yet to be seen. Even when the earth had become still, the fires that had broken out all over the city continued to rage. Firemen careening through the rubble-strewn streets on their horse-drawn engines were hard put to find a hydrant or water main that had not been disabled by the convulsions. They could do nothing to save the scores of people trapped inside burning buildings.

Eugene Schmitz, mayor of the city, ordered that dynamite be used to blow up buildings in order to stem the spread of fire. Brigadier-General Frederick F. Funston ordered out the army and sent an urgent telegram to Washington: "San Francisco practically destroyed. You cannot send too many tents and rations. 200,000 homeless."

It wasn't until Friday that the fire was finally brought under control. By then 25,000 buildings had been destroyed and nearly five hundred people had perished amid the ruins.

But President Theodore Roosevelt declared that San Francisco would rise again, and rise again it did, until today it is one of America's most prosperous and beautiful cities. However, deep beneath the Fisherman's Wharf and the Golden Gate Bridge there lies a giant rift in the earth that could someday bring about a grim reenactment of the 1906 catastrophe!

ON A WARM NIGHT IN AUGUST 1959 A TERRIBLE EARTHQUAKE SHOOK YELLOWSTONE NATIONAL PARK, SENDING 44 MILLION CUBIC YARDS OF EARTH AND ROCK POURING DOWN A MOUNTAINSIDE ONTO A FOREST SERVICE CAMPGROUND. NINETEEN CAMPERS WERE CRUSHED BENEATH THE SLIDE!

A Year of Terror

On the night of October 18, 1356, the inhabitants of the Swiss city of Basel were shaken from their sleep by a dreadful earthquake. The convulsions of the earth leveled every house, castle and church in every village for seventeen miles! Many people were able to escape to the countryside, with only a few hundred caught in the crumbling buildings of the towns and villages. A raging fire swept through their ruined homes as the survivors watched in horror. The aftershocks of the quake continued for more than a year afterwards!

Only about five earthquakes every year result in great destruction and loss of life. The rest—*nearly a million of them every year*—are only mild tremors often not detectable without instruments.

The ancient city of Antioch was ruined by earthquakes *nine times!* And earthquakes have brought disaster to Istanbul on *twelve* separate occasions since the days of the Roman Empire!

The River Ran Backwards!

In 1811 and 1812 a series of earthquake shocks struck New Madrid, Missouri, and played absolute havoc with nature!

Both banks of the Mississippi River caved in at one place and forced the water to flow upstream for a time!

THE **LIGHT** OF DESTRUCTION!

BEFORE A DEVASTATING EARTHQUAKE STRUCK TANGSHAN, CHINA IN 1976, THE NIGHT SKY **GLOWED WITH A BRIGHT LIGHT**-- AND **AFTER** THE QUAKE BUSHES APPEARED TO BE BURNT ON ONE SIDE, AND TREES WERE SQUASHED ABSOLUTELY FLAT AGAINST THE GROUND!

A forest area in Tennessee dropped twenty feet and surrounding waters drained into it, forming what is known today as Reelfoot Lake. The dead trunks of the drowned trees protruded above the water for many years.

An area of land fifteen miles long was lifted as much as twenty feet into the air! In Kentucky, the famed naturalist John James Audubon observed the ground undulating like waves at sea. Trees were bent down to the earth and their branches sometimes became entangled in the boughs of neighboring trees. When the trees straightened up, their branches remained entwined!

And in New Madrid itself, huge cracks opened in the ground. The local residents, terrified of falling into one of them, soon noticed that the fissures all ran in the same direction. So they cut down trees and laid them at right angles to the cracks. When the earth trembled anew, they leapt onto the tree trunks for safety!

The Lost Atlantis

According to the writings of Plato, the Greek philosopher and historian, there was once a large island called Atlantis which was shattered by a great earthquake and then entirely swallowed up by the ocean. For centuries, men have wondered whether Atlantis ever really existed, or was nothing more than a legend.

Today, some scientists believe that the ancient stories of the lost Atlantis actually refer to the devastation of a different island, an island called Santorin in the Aegean Sea. In 1470 B.C., Santorin was

WHEN AN **EARTHQUAKE** STRUCK LONDON IN 1750, ONE FAST-THINKING CON MAN FOUND A WAY TO MAKE MONEY FROM THE DISASTER --*HE SOLD PILLS* THAT HE CLAIMED WOULD PROTECT PEOPLE FROM *BEING HURT* BY THE QUAKE !

shaken by two serious earthquakes. The 30,000 residents of the town of Akrotiri quickly gathered up their belongings and fled—just before the island volcano exploded with a mighty blast burying the town under a mountain of black ash and submerging a large part of the island in the ocean forever. Massive tsunamis tore into the coastal cities all around Crete, and the great Minoan culture that had flourished there was instantly obliterated.

The Great Splash

Fishermen in the Gulf of Alaska consider the Lituya Bay a safe haven from stormy seas, but three fishing boats that took shelter there on the night of July 9, 1958, encountered instead a mighty wave that surged higher than any tsunami ever recorded!

Just after 10 P.M., a strong earthquake hit the area, shaking loose 90,000,000 tons of rock from the cliffs above Lituya Bay. The gigantic splash sent a wall of water *hundreds of feet high* charging across the bay at over one hundred miles per hour! Two of the boats were smashed to pieces, but the third successfully rode the crest of the wave over the tops of tall trees!

When the monster wave hit the opposite shore of the bay, it surged upwards to a height of *1740 feet* and cleared all the timber from an area covering almost *four square miles!*

Man-made Quake

Engineers and scientists have learned a tragic lesson—constructing an artificial lake can create seismic pressures in the earth's crust, pressures that can trigger a deadly quake!

In 1962, the Koyna Dam was built in an area of India considered by geologists to be especially stable. But as the level of the water rose in the reservoir, minor quakes began to occur. And then, on December 10, 1967, a major earthquake with a magnitude of 6.4 struck. The nearby town of Koyna Nagar was reduced to ruins, 177 of its residents were killed and 2300 more were injured!

Animal Earthquake Detectors

Today, we rely on seismographs and other sensitive instruments to warn us of impending earthquakes. But for many centuries, in many different regions of the world, people relied on animals to detect the signs of an approaching tremor. In some especially earthquake-prone areas, dogs and cats were kept specifically for that purpose. The animals would grow uneasy, and the dogs would howl all night before a shock was felt. It was thought at the time that the animals were gifted with a sixth sense when, in fact, they were only using their normal senses.

Many animals can detect sounds and movements that cannot be perceived by their human masters. They can feel and hear a subterranean rumbling long before the earth is rent apart. Before the Chilean city of Talcuhuana was struck by an earthquake in 1835, all the dogs had deserted the town. And when the French Riviera was threatened in 1887, horses all over the area refused to eat and tried to break out of their stalls. Even the birds in the trees fluttered about in a frenzy.

PIRATES' HAVEN

PORT ROYAL IN THE WEST INDIES WAS THE FAVORITE HARBOR OF BUCCANEERS UNTIL JUNE 7, 1692, WHEN AN EARTHQUAKE AND SEISMIC SEA WAVE *SWALLOWED* THE TOWN, KILLING **APPROXIMATELY 2,000 PEOPLE**! FOR A HUNDRED YEARS AFTER, MUCH OF THE TOWN *COULD BE SEEN UNDER 40 FEET OF WATER!*

It will be many years before the tragic summer of 1973 is forgotten in Mexico. The country had barely recovered from a powerful hurricane and a long month of heavy rains when a terrible earthquake struck! The strongest Mexico had felt in decades, the quake killed well over 500 people and injured 1000 more!

Shock Waves

In many public aquaria, the fish tanks bear warnings to visitors not to touch the glass because the vibrations can be harmful to many of the ultra-sensitive species. Imagine then the devastating effect of shock waves from an earthquake. Traveling through the open sea to shore, thousands of fish in coastal areas are killed. After the 1887 earthquake on the French Riviera, for example, huge numbers of dead fish floated up on the beaches around Nice.

The First Earthquake Detector

Earthquakes, of course, have been around since the dawn of time, but it wasn't until the year 132 A.D. that a Chinese inventor came up with a means of detecting them even when they were too far away to be felt. Chang Heng, the director of the Chinese Bureau of Almanac and History, devised the world's first seismoscope, an instrument that looked like an enormous wine bottle and stood eight feet tall. Chang Heng claimed that of eight strategically placed metal balls inside the instru-

FAMED OPERA TENOR,
ENRICO CARUSO, RAN THROUGH THE RUBBLE OF THE
1906 SAN FRANCISCO EARTHQUAKE, A TOWEL
AROUND HIS THROAT, CLUTCHING AN **AUTOGRAPHED
PICTURE OF TEDDY ROOSEVELT**!

WHEN THE ALASKAN EARTHQUAKE OF 1964 STRUCK, BALAS ERVIN LOOKED THROUGH A WINDOW TO SEE THE EARTH OUTSIDE **SUDDENLY SHOOT UPWARDS 50 FEET!** <u>A FISSURE HAD OPENED DIRECTLY BENEATH THE HOUSE</u> AND PLUNGED IT TO THE BOTTOM OF A CREVASSE!

LUCKILY HE ESCAPED--AND EVEN HELPED OTHERS TO <u>SURVIVE THIS GREATEST AMERICAN EARTHQUAKE EVER RECORDED!</u>

ment one would drop if an earthquake occurred, but no one believed him.

Then one day a ball did drop, though no one in the vicinity of the seismoscope had felt even the slightest tremor. It wasn't until ten days later that a messenger came with word that an earthquake had struck a far Western province! Chang Heng was rewarded for his astonishing invention with a job as secretary in charge of monitoring and studying earthquakes!

Hurricanes
and Tornadoes

The Hurricane That Helped Discover America

For days, a steady wind had been blowing the *Nina,* the *Pinta* and the *Santa Maria* westward in their voyage of discovery and the crew worried that the constant westerly wind would make it impossible to return home. When the winds abruptly stopped one day and the ships floated on a still sea, the sailors panicked and plotted a mutiny. They might actually have carried it out were it not for the heavy waves that the lookout saw stretching out as far as the horizon. The rough seas convinced the sailors there would be wind enough in this uncharted region to carry them back to Spain.

Today, scientists surmise that the heavy swells were the result of a mighty hurricane situated many miles away from Columbus's fleet. If the storm had come closer, America might have had to wait many more years to be discovered!

The Labor Day hurricane of 1935 wasn't very impressive when it comes to size—but it was the most intensely concentrated and powerful storm ever recorded! Its barometer reading was only 26.35—the lowest ever registered—and its winds were clocked at *over 200 miles per hour!* On the night of September 2 it slammed into the Florida Keys, and by dawn 400 people were dead!

WHEN HURRI-CANE WINDS SMASHED INTO SO. CAROLINA IN 1893, BLOWING HUNDREDS TO THEIR DEATH, MANY FAST-THINKING RESIDENTS SAVED THEMSELVES BY *LASHING THEIR BODIES TO STRONG TREES!*

Living Sacrifice to Hunraken

In the ancient Mayan culture of Central America, the greatest god of all was the sun god, but just below him was the god of the storm, Hunraken—from which we have derived our term "hurricane" today. To appease the storm god's angry temper, and ensure a plentiful rainfall, the Mayans made an annual sacrifice. A beautiful maiden was chosen by the high priests and for many months she was honored. But at the end of her brief celebrity, she was escorted to the lip of a huge limestone sinkhole and there thrown to her death. A brave young warrior leapt in after her, to serve as her protector as she journeyed to the distant realm of Hunraken. Jubilant spectators cast precious objects of art and gold into the sacred waters to further ingratiate themselves with the dangerously temperamental god.

The most murderous cyclone ever recorded wreaked havoc in the Bay of Bengal area on October 7, 1737. Sweeping over the delta of the River Ganges, the cyclone destroyed 20,000 boats and produced a 40 foot high wave that flooded whole islands and thousands of acres of lowlands. *300,000 people* lost their lives to the cyclone's deadly fury.

Central New England is seldom the victim of hurricane winds, but for almost two weeks in 1938 the entire New England area was battered by an extremely powerful storm. *Two hundred seventy five million trees* were uprooted, hundreds of millions of dollars in property damage was done, and 600 New Englanders were killed.

STORM WAR!

AFTER THE UNITED STATES THIRD FLEET LOST 3 DESTROYERS AND NEARLY 800 MEN IN A PHILIPPINES TYPHOON ON DEC.17, 1944, THE U.S. NAVY STARTED STUDYING WAYS OF **STEERING TYPHOONS TOWARD ENEMY SHIPS!**

CHILDREN WERE WHISKED INTO THE AIR -- CAUGHT IN THE VACUUM OF A TORNADO THAT HIT WORCESTER, MASS. --AND HAD TO BE DRAGGED BACK TO EARTH BY THEIR FRANTIC MOTHERS!

(1953)

The Birds' Eye

The eye of a hurricane is the relatively calm interior around which the deadly winds circulate. Our feathered friends often hitch a ride in the eye of a storm and travel far from their natural habitats. After a Caribbean hurricane hit the East Coast of America, tropical birds were found perched on trees in New England—2000 miles away from their island home!

Costliest Disaster Ever!

Hurricane Agnes battered the Eastern U.S. for four days in the summer of 1972—taking *118 lives* and leaving property damage of over *THREE BILLION DOLLARS!*

What a Catch!

In some towns along the Gulf Coast, the local fishermen haven't even had to go fishing to catch fish—the fish have just dropped down out of the sky! They're the surprise gift of a waterspout—a tornado that has formed over the sea. Sometimes, whole schools of small fish are sucked up into the vortex of the waterspout, and then dumped *en masse* when the funnel cloud begins to pass over land. Waterspouts have also been known to pick up hordes of frogs and tadpoles and rain them down on an inland region!

SUNKEN TREASURE!

IN 1715 A VICIOUS CYCLONE SANK A SPANISH ARMADA, LOADED WITH TREASURE JUST A FEW YARDS OFF THE COAST OF FLORIDA. MILLIONS OF DOLLARS WORTH OF **GOLD AND SILVER STILL REMAIN THERE TO BE SALVAGED!**

The Cyclone That Started a Nation

More than one half million East Pakistanis died in the turmoil of a massive cyclone in 1970. Subjected to indifference from the government, they revolted, declaring the independent state of Bangladesh!

THE **DEADLY WINDS** OF HURRICANE CAMILLE GUSTING *TO OVER 200 MILES PER HOUR* DROVE A 10-FOOT LONG WOODEN PLANK STRAIGHT THROUGH THE TRUNK OF A ROYAL PALM TREE!

May Day

For the little Kansas town of Codell, May 20th was a date they could do without. On that day in 1916 a tornado ripped into the town. On the same day, one year later, another tornado hit the city. And on May 20th, 1918, Codell was ravaged by a third tornado! And they each hit at about the same time of day!

An Uninvited Mourner

On September 23, 1834, the people of a town in Santo Domingo went to the village church to attend the funeral of a beloved priest, Padre Ruiz. No sooner had the services begun than a vicious hurricane hit the island destroying homes, sinking ships, and taking many lives. Forever after, that terrible hurricane has been called the "Padre Ruiz."

Shakespeare's "Bermoothes" Storm

We often wonder where great writers get their inspiration. Well, William Shakespeare once got his from a hurricane!

In 1609, a fleet of nine ships was on its way from Plymouth, England, to Jamestown, Virginia, when a fierce hurricane suddenly swept down upon them, sinking one of the ships and dispersing the others. Seven finally limped into port in Virginia, but the eighth was presumed lost at sea.

LAST DANCE!

DESPITE A RAGING HURRICANE, 400 GUESTS WERE ENJOYING AN ELEGANT BALL OFF THE COAST OF LOUISIANA ON LAST ISLAND IN 1856 — **WHEN THE BALLROOM CRUMBLED** AND **HUNDREDS** OF THEM WERE SWEPT IN THEIR FINERY INTO THE ANGRY SEA!

But the ship had not gone down after all; instead, it had run aground on the island of Bermuda. The passengers and crewmen who survived the shipwreck immediately set to work building vessels to continue their journey, and after nine months they again set sail, arriving safely in Jamestown almost a year late.

Two of the men who had landed in Bermuda later recounted their island adventures in vivid detail. Their accounts became popular reading of the day, and it is almost certain that Shakespeare read them, for his play entitled "The Tempest" draws heavily on their descriptions of the hurricane and the island of Bermuda. Without these accounts—and the storm—we might never have had one of Shakespeare's great and enduring plays!

"Rain of Blood!"

In certain areas of America, the horrified residents have reported what they believed to be a "rain of blood"—red rainfalls! What they had in fact witnessed was the long-range effect of a tornado! As much as a hundred miles away, a tornado had passed over an area of red clay and picked up billions of clay particles into its storm clouds. These particles mixed with the water droplets in the upper atmosphere and fell to earth in an errie red rain!

THE EASTERN SEABOARD HURRICANE OF 1938 DAMAGED OR UTTERLY <u>DESTROYED</u> 6,923 CHURCHES ALONG THE U.S. COAST-- BUT STRANGELY ENOUGH, *SPARED ALL THE SYNAGOGUES AND EPISCOPAL CHURCHES !*

SUNK BY A VICIOUS HURRICANE ON DECEMBER 24, 1811, TWO BRITISH SHIPS PARTIALLY **RESURFACED**, REVEALING THE GRIM SPECTACLE OF **OVER 500 DROWNED SAILORS LITTERING THE DECKS** !

The Typhoon That Made Peace

After a German fleet bombed American property in Samoa in March, 1889, three United States warships quickly arrived on the scene. Battle was imminent, but a sudden typhoon swept into the harbor and destroyed all the German and American ships before they could open hostilities. Without any means of waging war, the countries had to make a peace agreement.

In June, 1934, a hurricane struck the country of Honduras in Central America. Torrential rains fell, and the Ulua River began to rise dangerously. The people of Pimienta, a town built on the very edge of the river, fled to the top of a small hill nearby. But the rains continued, and the waters rose. Around the hill covered with frightened refugees the waters gradually mounted the slope. Up and up the waters climbed, until the hill was overwhelmed and all the villagers of Pimienta drowned!

A Brutal Introduction

Many of the people living in Miami in 1926 were new to the area. They'd come down with the Florida land boom and they had no idea of the havoc a hurricane could wreak. Even when the hurricane warning flags went up at the municipal docks on September 17th, not many took precautions. Soon the deadly hurricane that had been born near the Cape Verde Islands, swept across the Atlantic and was suddenly upon them!

HAPPY LANDING

A TORNADO THAT STRUCK EL DORADO, KANSAS, IN 1958 SUCKED A WOMAN THROUGH A WINDOW, SWEPT HER **60 FEET THROUGH THE AIR** AND DROPPED HER <u>UNHARMED</u> NEXT TO A BROKEN RECORD OF *"STORMY WEATHER!"*

AUDREY, THE POISONOUS HURRICANE!

OVER **500** PEOPLE PERISHED WHEN HURRICANE AUDREY LASHED INTO LOUISIANA AND TEXAS IN JUNE, 1957— MANY WERE CAUGHT UP IN THE VIOLENT WINDS AND TERRIBLE FLOODS, *AND ONE CHILD EVEN DIED OF A SNAKEBITE* WHEN VENOMOUS REPTILES AND TOADS--EVEN ALLIGATORS--WERE BLOWN ONTO CITY STREETS!

For nearly two days, the city of Miami was battered and torn by screaming winds that reached 128 miles per hour, winds that ripped the roofs off houses and hurled deadly debris through the streets. Witnesses recalled seeing a cow flying through the air, with a man hanging on to its tail! The Myer-Kiser Bank Building, fourteen stories high, had been twisted out of shape by the violent winds, and the enormous wave that had swept across Biscayne Bay had lifted a hugh ship right out of the water and plunked it down across from the *Daily News* Tower! There it stayed. Years later, it was turned into an aquarium and became a prime tourist attraction!

A Pack of Troubles

For the people of Charleston, South Carolina, finishing their breakfasts and on their way to work, it was one morning they would never be able to forget. *Five* separate tornadoes suddenly slammed into the town and left thirty-two people dead in their wake, along with another 150 injured. Two million dollars worth of property damage was done.

But tornadoes have often been known to roam in deadly packs. In 1952, a flock of *thirty-one* twisters tore into six states from Missouri to Alabama and killed 343 people! Over 3500 homes were utterly destroyed and the damages were assessed at fifteen million dollars!

THE **TOWN TORNADOES LOVED!**

ON MARCH 16, 1942 BALDWYN, MISS., WAS ATTACKED
BY **2 SEPARATE TORNADOES**--ONLY **25 MINUTES APART!**
65 PEOPLE DIED, MOST OF THEM HAVING LEFT THEIR
SHELTERS AFTER THE FIRST ONSLAUGHT--ONLY TO
BE CAUGHT UNAWARES BY THE *SECOND SAVAGE
STORM OF THE DAY* !

AFTER RIDING OUT A HURRICANE FOR HOURS IN HIS 32-FOOT CABIN CRUISER, DAVID POTTS OF WEST-HAMPTON BEACH, N.Y., DROPPED ANCHOR-- ONLY TO DISCOVER, WHEN THE WATERS RECEDED, THAT HE *HAD DOCKED ON THE FRONT LAWN OF A HOME!*

Double-Barreled Menace

One of the most treacherous freaks of nature is the concealment of a tornado *inside* a hurricane! From time to time it happens—and on September 10, 1919, it happened to the town of Goulds, Florida. The secret tornado tore into the city, ripping off roofs and folding them around the trunks of trees thousands of yards away!

Oops!

For years, scientists had wondered about the possibility of draining a hurricane's destructive fury by "seeding" it—that is, by impregnating its clouds with chemicals that would help to release some of its heat energy.

In 1947 the first attempt was made. The target hurricane was traveling in a northerly direction along the Eastern coast of the United States. A single plane flew into its cloud banks and scattered 200 pounds of dry ice. Shortly thereafter, the storm made an abrupt turn to the west and tore into Georgia!

While government authorities later claimed the seeding was not responsible for the hurricane's change of course, there were many who contended otherwise. As a result, the government drew up extensive rules and regulations in 1962 to clarify where and when modification experiments on hurricanes could safely be performed.

4

Floods
and Tsunami

The Johnstown Flood

For years, the people living near the Conemaugh and Stoneycreek rivers had endured the spring floods. When the rivers overflowed, they routinely abandoned the first floor of their homes and moved upstairs. But in the spring of 1889 unusually heavy snowstorms were followed by unusually heavy rains. The waters poured into the Conemaugh Lake reservoir and created enormous pressures on its clay and shale dam.

In the little town of South Fork, nestled in the valley below the reservoir, word of the danger went out and the people escaped to higher ground. But the telegraph lines to Johnstown were down and there was no way to alert the people to the potential disaster.

In just a few fatal seconds the huge dam burst apart, spilling five billion gallons of water down into the valley. A wall of water forty feet high leveled South Fork, and moved on to the towns, factories and railway yards below it. The Philadelphia and New York express train was snatched up by the rushing waters and smashed to pieces. Only eleven passengers survived.

The flood continued down the valley, filled with heavy debris. It pulverized everything in its path

THE **MURDEROUS FLOOD** THAT OBLITERATED JOHNSTOWN, PA. IN 1889 KILLING THOUSANDS, SPARED ONE 5-MONTH-OLD INFANT WHO **SAILED ALL THE WAY TO PITTSBURGH**, 75 MILES AWAY, *ON THE FLOORBOARDS OF A RUINED HOME!*

and only came to a temporary halt behind the great Stone Bridge at Johnstown. Here the mighty wall of wreckage formed a new dam of sorts, a dam built of broken homes and twisted railroad cars. While hundreds of people were ensnared in the tangled mass, petroleum spilled from a tank car and suddenly was ignited by a stove. The flames leaped through the mountain of wreckage and burned more than three hundred people unable to get free. The fire blazed for three days.

The flood itself swept onward into Johnstown, where the rampaging waters tore almost every house loose from its foundations. The people tried desperately to cling to roofs and floating debris, but it was nearly impossible to hold on in the dark, madly swirling waters. By the time the deadly flood had passed through Johnstown, virtually nothing was left of the town that had once been home to eighteen thousand people. The survivors had lost everything they owned in the world, and 2500 others had lost their lives.

No Escape

After the Japanese town of Tugaru was hit by a severe earthquake in 1793, the tsunami that resulted from it sucked the water away from the shore, leaving the beach exposed. But the townspeople had seen this strange effect before, and instead of going down to the shoreline, they retreated to high ground. They *knew* the wave would return! But before it did, the ground suddenly shook again, and in terror the people ran from the heights, down to the relative safety of the broad, flat beach. They

GENTLE GIANT

A **TSUNAMI**, OR MIGHTY SEA WAVE, THAT HIT THE HAWAIIAN ISLAND OF OAHU IN 1946, LIFTED A HOUSE OFF ITS FOUNDATION, SWEPT IT **200 FEET INLAND**, AND DEPOSITED IT IN A CANE FIELD WITH THE *BREAKFAST STILL SIMMERING ON THE STOVE!*

RAMPAGING FLOOD WATERS

ENVELOPED EDGEMONT, OHIO, IN 1913! CAUGHT IN THE STREET, FLOSSIE LESTER THOUGHT FAST— *SHE JUMPED ABOARD A HORSE-DRAWN VAN, AND WHEN THE ROILING WATERS CAUGHT UP TO IT AND THE HORSES BROKE THEIR HARNESS, SHE SWAM AFTER THEM, MOUNTED ONE, AND RODE IT TO SAFETY A MILE AND A HALF AWAY!*

had no sooner arrived there than the killer wave swept forward from the sea, a mighty wall of churning water that crushed and drowned them!

Deadly Downpour

In July, 1829, the Inverness area of Great Britain was hit by torrential rains. But the water droplets didn't fall like normal precipitation. Instead, the region was virtually engulfed in an impenetrable mist of tiny water particles, the thick sea of falling moisture was so heavy that birds and small animals were literally pelted to death beneath it! The staggering downpour swelled the mountain streams and rivers to overflowing, and great floods of water rushed down the Scottish valleys toward the small towns below. Everything in the path of the water was destroyed; a gigantic wave broke a stone arch over sixty feet high from a bridge and bore it aloft for quite some distance before the arch finally crumbled to pieces!

The Disappearing Island

Uryû-jima, a small island off the coast of Japan, was once home to five thousand people. But on September 4, 1596, it was hit by a single earthquake shock. The ground was torn open in places, and several buildings were damaged. That seemed to be the extent of the earthquake—until a tsunami suddenly slammed into the island, drowning more than seven hundred people. By the next morning,

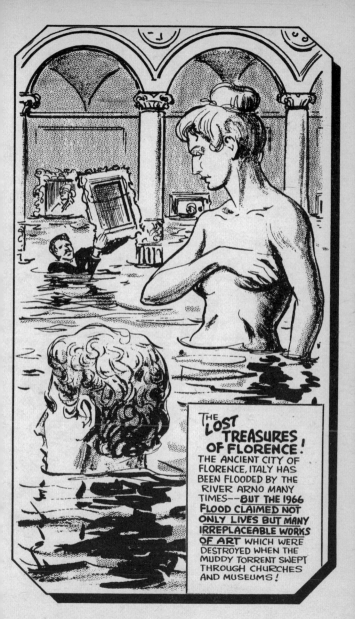

THE **LOST TREASURES** OF FLORENCE! THE ANCIENT CITY OF FLORENCE, ITALY HAS BEEN FLOODED BY THE RIVER ARNO MANY TIMES--*BUT THE 1966 FLOOD CLAIMED NOT ONLY LIVES BUT MANY IRREPLACEABLE WORKS OF ART* WHICH WERE DESTROYED WHEN THE MUDDY TORRENT SWEPT THROUGH CHURCHES AND MUSEUMS!

PRIDE BEFORE LIFE!
A BUS BELIEVED TO BE CARRYING MEMBERS OF 2 DIFFERENT INDIAN CASTES WAS WASHED INTO A RAMPAGING RIVER... 78 PEOPLE DROWNED RATHER THAN SHARE THE SINGLE LIFELINE TO SHORE!

WAVE of DESTRUCTION!

RESIDENTS OF SANRIKU, JAPAN, WATCHED IN HORROR AS A MASSIVE WAVE **GLOWING WITH A BRIGHT LIGHT** RUSHED TOWARD SHORE AT **500** MILES PER HOUR! THE MIGHTY WAVE, **WHICH HAD CHURNED UP HORDES OF PHOSPHORESCENT OCEAN CREATURES**, SANK 8,000 SHIPS AND DROWNED THOUSANDS OF PEOPLE!

LEAVE IT TO BEAVERS! ON SEPT. 22, 1938 60 BEAVER COLONIES IN STONY POINT, N.Y. FOUGHT BACK RAMPAGING FLOOD WATERS, SAVING MAJOR HIGHWAYS, BRIDGES AND HUNDREDS OF ACRES OF VALUABLE LAND. THEIR DAMS MEASURED UP TO **600 FEET** LONG AND **FOURTEEN FEET THICK!**

FLOODS ON THE SAHARA?

ON NOVEMBER 27, 1962 AN OASIS OVERFLOWED ON THE DESERT'S EDGE IN SOUTHERN TUNISIA FLOODING HOMES AND TAKING APPROXIMATELY **40 LIVES**!

most of the island had dropped underwater. As time passed, the rest followed, until the entire island of Uryû-jima resided on the ocean floor, thirty fathoms deep.

Fatal Alert

After the Hawaiian city of Hilo was devastated by a tsunami in 1946, an ingenious warning system was devised to spot these monstrous waves before they hit land. Ironically, it was the warning system itself which resulted in the loss of many lives in 1962! Thousands of people, alerted to an approaching wave, flocked to the beaches to see it! Sixty-one people were killed, and nearly three hundred more were injured!

China's Sorrow . . .

. . . that's what they call the Hwang Ho River. It floods more often than any river in the world and presents a constant menace to the millions of peasants who must nevertheless use it to irrigate their crops. In September and October of 1887, the Hwang Ho River washed over its 70-foot levees and drowned almost one million Chinese!

Never Say Die

Leveled by a massive tidal wave in September 1900 that killed 6000 people, *the whole city* of Galveston, Texas, was *raised 17 feet above sea level* and was *totally rebuilt!*

Weather
Disasters

The Blizzard of '88

It was March 11, 1888, and the inhabitants of New York City went about their daily business without an inkling of the terrible snowstorm that was about to descend upon them. Before it was spent it would claim 200 lives and destroy an estimated twenty million dollars in property!

One of the unsuspecting victims was a man named George D. Baremore, who woke up on Monday morning and prepared to go to his office. When a policeman at his train station told him the snow and gale-force winds had stopped all service, Baremore stubbornly set off for the next station three blocks away. It was only a few hours later that two policemen discovered him frozen to death in a snowdrift!

Every year, lightning bolts crashing to earth cause millions of dollars in property damage and take hundreds of lives in the U.S. alone!

To get some idea of its potential for destruction, in a split second a single flash of lightning can expend 250 kilowatt hours of energy—enough power to raise the huge *S.S. United States* six feet above the ground!

DEEP FREEZE!

3 WOMEN, BURIED IN A RUINED STABLE UNDER A 60-FOOT DEEP AVALANCHE OF SNOW, SURVIVED FOR **37 DAYS** IN A HOLE **12** FEET LONG AND **5** FEET HIGH. WHEN RESCUED, ONE HAD LOST HER POWER OF SPEECH AND ANOTHER ALL HER HAIR!
(Stura Valley, Italy. March 1775)

Continents in Collision

Forget the old saying, "firm as the earth beneath your feet." It may seem stable, but the ground is in fact always moving. In the course of your own lifetime, the United States and Europe will move six feet farther apart. Hawaii will crawl northward, and Los Angeles will creep ten feet closer to San Francisco.

Geologists believe that the face of the earth eventually will be drastically altered. Africa and South America will be a thousand miles farther away from each other than they are today, and Australia will smack into Indonesia. India will continue to burrow under part of Asia and drive the Himalayas' even higher. Great slabs of Africa will break off and float free, as will a slice of California with Los Angeles riding on it.

Least you panic about these dire predictions, keep in mind that scientists have allotted *fifty million years* for these drastic changes to occur! So relax.

Our Poisoned Atmosphere

Everyday, we further pollute the blanket of air that surrounds our planet by filling it with waste fumes from our factories, automobiles, airplanes. And some scientists contend that the constant build-up of carbon dioxide in the atmosphere poses a serious threat to the survival of the earth. They maintain that the carbon dioxide density may eventually become so great that it will act as a kind of mirror, reflecting solar radiation back into space rather than allowing it to warm the earth. If that happens, another Ice Age could begin and spell the end to the world as we now know it.

Other scientists, however, predict an altogether different, if equally grim, conclusion. They believe that the carbon dioxide layer will actually *trap* radiation on earth, raising the surface temperature over a hundred degrees! Venus, they point out, registers a surface temperature of 800 degrees Fahrenheit, most probably as a result of the planet's thick atmosphere which keeps the heat from escaping into space.

The Emotional Toll

Sometimes people only feel the personal effects of an earthquake, tornado or other disaster long after the immediate danger has passed. In the following weeks, and even months, many of those who lived through the destruction have trouble eating and sleeping; they experience nausea, fear, and sometimes even lose their hair. The nightmarish scenes they witnessed haunt some disaster victims for a lifetime.

It was all over in a few seconds. A dreadful avalanche of rocks and ice that swept down on the villages at the foot of a narrow valley in Peru. In an instant, a mountain of earth and debris had totally buried the towns and thousands of their inhabitants forever.

According to the village records of Widdecombe-

UNEXPECTED ICY FOE!

JUST BEFORE AN ATTACK ON THE FRENCH, **OVER 1,000 KNIGHTS** IN THE ARMY OF ENGLAND'S EDWARD III WERE SLAUGHTERED **BY A RAIN OF DEADLY HAIL!**

on-the-Moor in Devon, England, the town church was once, long ago, "visited by the devil!"

While services were in progress, a terrible thunderstorm struck, suddenly changing the day to night. The unearthly blackness was broken only by flashes of lightning, accompanied by blasts of thunder. Suddenly, a bolt of lightning hit the church itself, filling the interior with smoke and a sulfurous smell. Before the terrified worshipers could escape, a ball of fire appeared in a window of the church and floated inside. The people threw themselves to the floor crying and praying for deliverance as the fiery ball slowly passed through the church.

After it had disappeared, it was discovered that four people had been killed and another sixty-two injured. Many more had had articles of clothing burnt right off their bodies!

Bleak Decade

According to statistics complied by the Red Cross, the United States took a greater battering from natural disasters during the 1950s than during any comparable recorded period. Over *3000* natural disasters occurred in those ten years, and over *a million and a half Americans* were temporarily—or permanently—uprooted!

Deadly Heat Wave

Crops withered in the fields. Fires raged unchecked through vast forest lands. The water level of the Great Lakes sank over a foot. During the summer

AT A GERMAN GLIDING EXHIBITION, 5 PILOTS STEERED THEIR PLANES **INTO A MASSIVE THUNDERCLOUD,** HOPING THE WINDS WOULD BOOST THEM HIGHER. BUT WHEN THE STORM THREATENED TO DESTROY THE PLANES, **THEY BAILED OUT** — INTO AN ICY UPDRAFT THAT CARRIED THEM ALOFT AND KEPT THEM THERE, **UNTIL ALL BUT ONE HAD FROZEN TO DEATH** ... **IN A COAT OF ICE!**

months of 1934, the Midwestern portion of the United States suffered its worst drought in recorded history. Temperatures exceeded 100 degrees Fahrenheit during the daylight hours, while the nights didn't drop below 80 degrees. Just during August, 1500 lives were lost to the dreadful heat and heat-related complications.

It was this dry and stifling era that turned a large region of the country into what has come to be known as the "Dust Bowl."

The Dangerous Fiords

The people of Norway have more to fear than their icy winters. Those who live near the mighty fiords, deep chasms cut by huge glaciers, must live in dread of sudden landslides. Tons of rock and debris, plunging into the waters of the fiord, can create enormous waves that ruin homes and take many lives! Time and again, Norwegian villagers living near the Innvik Fiord have suffered the tragic onslaught of these waves. In 1905 and 1936, landslides spilled into the icy lake below and threw up deadly waves that rushed inland, sweeping away homes and killing over a hundred people! The power of one wave was so great that it carried a steamship a quarter of a mile inland!

Founded on Salt

For centuries, Venice has been known as the "Pride of the Adriatic." Built during the Middle Ages by the greatest artisans and architects of the day, Venice rests not on firm ground, but on many small islands formed by silt deposits. Venice's wealth was based on salt, the most priceless commodity known to man and a medium of exchange for over seven centuries. Salt made the city powerful and strengthened the treasury, resulting in the creation of one of the world's most unique and magnificent cities, where canals are used in place of streets and transportation is by gondola. Today, however, *the city is sinking,* while even the best engineers and scientists are hard put to find a way to keep this city of unparalleled beauty from nestling down further into the soft ground on which it rests.

The Stealthy Menace

"The fog comes on little cat feet," wrote poet Carl Sandburg. But that image belies its often disastrous effects. Fog blinds the drivers of cars, and makes navigation a much more hazardous affair for planes and ships. In one year alone (1965-1966), insurance companies declared that in the United States fog had been the cause of 1000 deaths and fifty to sixty thousand injuries!

During the First World War, an invisible enemy— the wind—defeated the German Air Force. On a bombing raid on London, the German planes were caught in a powerful northeast wind that blew them relentlessly toward French lines, where they were shot to pieces by anti-aircraft fire!

It was long believed that the ringing of church bells could divert the fury of a storm—despite all evi-

THE ANCIENT "LIGHTNING ROD"!
THE ANCIENT ROMANS BELIEVED THE LAUREL PLANT OFFERED PROTECTION AGAINST **LIGHTNING BOLTS** -- AND THE EMPEROR TIBERIUS, **TERRIFIED OF THUNDERSTORMS,** ALWAYS KEPT A LAUREL WREATH WITHIN EASY REACH TO WEAR ON HIS HEAD IN CASE OF A STORM!

dence to the contrary. A book published in 1784 reported that lightning bolts had struck 386 church steeples in Germany—and killed over a hundred bell ringers!—in a 33 year span.

Landslides have long plagued the Japanese, so in 1971 a team from the Agency of Science and Technology decided to manufacture a landslide of their own, which they could photograph and study. TV crews and reporters were invited to attend the event. A steep hillside was sprayed with water from a nearby reservoir in order to simulate a torrential rain. But then, before anyone was prepared for it, the cliff suddenly gave way, spilling a huge mass of muddy earth down on the assembled scientists and reporters. Fifteen people were instantly killed and ten more injured by the manufactured landslide.

The Treacherous Alps

During the First World War, Italian and Austrian forces clashing in the Tyrol section of the Alps had more to worry about than each other. In one twenty-four-hour period, over 10,000 soldiers—in both armies—were killed by sudden, deadly avalanches!

In fact, *man-made* avalanches became a common weapon. Troops shelled the snowfields above their enemies and allowed the crushing tons of snow and ice to do their work for them. Between 1915 and 1918, it is estimated that as many as 60,000 soldiers lost their lives in the freezing Alps.

In 1926, the U.S. Navy's largest ammunition depot was located at Lake Denmark, New Jersey. An afternoon thunderstorm in July hurtled a lightning bolt earthward, where it started a fire that set off massive explosions in the depot. The blast killed *sixteen people,* threw debris a distance of *22 miles,* and destroyed a total of *70 million dollars* in property! It was the *costliest lightning bolt* in American history!

According to the ancient Greek historian Herodotus, an entire nation once perished when it attempted to wage war on the wind itself. A parching wind from the south had dried up all the water storage receptacles in the land of the Psylli. The people would soon die of thirst unless something were done about the unrelenting wind. The leaders of the Psylli anxiously met and decided to do battle with their impossible foe. Girding themselves for the fight, they marched into the desert, where the invincible wind from the south swept down over them and buried the Psylli soldiers under mountains of blowing sand.

It was January, 1922, and Washington, D.C. was being buried under twenty-eight inches of wet snow. The crushing weight of the snow was too great for the roof of the Knickerbocker movie theater, which suddenly buckled and spilled a murderous avalanche down on the people inside, killing ninety-six and injuring over a hundred more!

The Giant's Revenge

For years, the Swiss villagers had been digging away at the foot of the mighty peak that towered above their town. The mountain was a rich source of slate, and even after their extensive quarrying had caused the summit to crack dangerously the villagers continued to blast and dig.

And then, after a month of steady rain, the giant peak took its revenge. On September 11, 1881, a section of the mountain broke away and crashed down into the valley. The avalanche of rocks and debris stopped a few hundred yards short of the town's inn, and terrified residents scurried away. Only seventeen minutes later, a second landslide hurtled down on the village, pulverizing the inn and killing many people. But even that was not the end of it. A *third* fall, which came within minutes, was even more murderous than its predecessors. A rushing torrent of rocks and earth descended upon the town, hurling a strong wind before it that tore houses and trees to shreds. When the deadly avalanche at last subsided, the little Swiss town, and 115 of its inhabitants, had disappeared under ten million cubic yards of rock!

A Lost Civilization

By 1276 A.D., Indians in the American Southwest had created an extraordinary civilization. Judging from the remaining artifacts and architecture, they had attained a high degree of culture. But their society, like other early societies, was founded on agriculture, and when the rains didn't come, their crops withered and their water sources dried up. For twenty-three consecutive years, the American Southwest suffered from a severe drought, a drought which forced the Indians to abandon their pueblo homes and their cities built into the cliffs and go in search of water. Over the centuries, their deserted towns crumbled away and their once proud civilization was reduced to dust and ruins.

Lightning and Sports

Time and again, lightning bolts have wreaked havoc at sporting events!

In July, 1949, lightning struck a baseball diamond in Baker, Florida, tearing a hole in the infield twenty feet long! The shortstop and third baseman were killed instantly, the second baseman mortally wounded, and fifty spectators suffered injuries!

In 1959, two soccer players died and seventeen more were hurt when lightning struck a playing field in Brazil.

And England's famous Ascot race track was hit by lightning on July 14, 1955, with two people killed and 44 other injured!

Divine Protection

In the days before lightning rods and fire detectors, many people looked to a patron saint, Saint Barbara, for protection against thunder, lightning and fire.

Barbara herself had lived in the fourth century A.D., the daughter of a rich pagan. When he learned she had converted to Christianity, he became enraged and beheaded her. A moment later, he was hit by a bolt of lightning and killed on the spot!

For centuries, Greeks, Romans and Russians celebrated the anniversary of her martyrdom, December 4, with great feasts. And up until 1940, the Chief

IN 1769 THE CITY OF BRESCIA, ITALY, WAS UTTERLY DESTROYED--AND THOUSANDS OF ITS RESIDENTS KILLED-- WHEN A BOLT OF LIGHTNING STRUCK THE CHURCH OF ST. NAZAIRE AND EXPLODED *ONE HUNDRED TONS OF GUNPOWDER STORED IN ITS VAULTS!*

of the U.S. Navy Bureau of Ordnance—the man responsible for keeping artillery safe from fire and accidents—kept a painting of Saint Barbara in his Washington office.

According to legends circulated by the islanders in the South Pacific, there was once a land called Mu which, like the fabled continent of Atlantis, disappeared forever into the depths of the ocean. Easter Island was thought to be all that was left of Mu, and there was at least one strange bit of evidence that seemed to substantiate the story—paved roads on the island led straight down into the sea, and some natives believed that if the roads were followed, they would lead to the sunken Mu.

Unfortunately, the myths were fairly well disproven by the famed explorer Thor Heyerdahl who ordered a scuba diver to follow a road underwater. It only went a few feet before it stopped, leading the diver and Heyerdahl to surmise that the roads were simply ancient landing ramps for native boats. If the land of Mu did exist, it lies buried still, somewhere in the uncharted depths of the vast Pacific Ocean.

The Donner Disaster

Today, both U.S. 40 and the tracks of the Southern Pacific Railroad wend their way through the Donner Pass in the Sierra Nevada mountains. But the Donner Pass wasn't always so easily traveled. In November 1846 George Donner led a wagon train of Illinois pioneers up into the pass. Before they could get through it, a terrible blizzard struck and buried the wagons in deep, impenetrable snow-drifts. As the weeks—and months—wore on, the stranded pioneers struggled to survive. When their food supply ran out, some members of the party resorted to cannibalism, devouring those who had already succumbed to the cold or starvation! It wasn't until March of the following year that rescuers were able to reach the forty-three desperate survivors of the ill-fated Donner wagon train.

The most massive and dangerous cloud formation of all, the thunderhead, wields the power of an *atom bomb!* Its wild, tempestuous air currents can utterly destroy an aircraft—as the U.S. Navy learned on September 2, 1925.

It wasn't long after the dirigible *Shenandoah* had taken off from Lakehurst, New Jersey, that it flew into a fierce thunderstorm over the Ohio River Valley. The violent, swirling winds twisted the mighty ship out of shape and tore it into three separate pieces! Fourteen of the crew members perished in the crash!

Fires,
Explosions
and Collapses

Tragedy at the Cocoanut Grove

On the evening of November 28, 1942, nearly a thousand people were packed into a popular Boston nightclub, the Cocoanut Grove. Many of them were celebrating the surprise football victory of Holy Cross over Boston College; others were soldiers about to be shipped overseas. The Melody Lounge, a dark, romantic room downstairs in the club, was filled to overflowing when the first flames were seen. Caused by either a faulty electrical connection or a match lit by a busboy and accidentally touched to an artificial palm frond—no one will ever know for sure—the fire suddenly raced across the blue satin that covered the ceiling. Waiters and bartenders futilely tried to swat it out with wet rags and seltzer bottles. As the flames spread and smoke began to cloud the room, hundreds of revelers made a mad rush for the only stairway leading upstairs. They crushed and trampled each other underfoot, then jammed the main revolving door out of the club so that it would no longer turn.

By now, the raging fire had erupted into the upstairs ballroom and the new cocktail lounge. Billowing black smoke blinded and suffocated the customers as they staggered about in search of an exit. There were twelve doors out of the Cocoanut

113

Grove, but nine were locked that night and one had been blocked off. The choking people piled on top of each other as deadly fumes from the burning decorations in the club swirled through the blazing interior.

Firemen called to the scene had to fight their way past the crush of bodies just to get near the fire itself. When they entered the Melody Lounge, they found customers at the bar still holding their drinks, but their casual postures were deceptive. They had all been asphyxiated by the fumes. All tolled, the Cocoanut Grove fire claimed 491 lives, then making it the second most disastrous fire in U.S. history.

It was a beautiful, sunny afternoon at the Spanish seaside resort of San Carlos de la Rápita. Some 600 tourists—French, West German and Belgian— were relaxing around their tents and trailers, enjoying picnic lunches, or napping in the shade of the palm and cypress trees that fringed the beach. It was hard to imagine anything disturbing the tranquility of the afternoon. Suddenly a huge tanker truck filled with highly combustible propylene gas swung out of control on the highway that ran directly behind the campsite. It smashed into a retaining wall and exploded in a massive ball of fire! Flames hundreds of feet high swept across the beach, instantly igniting everything and everyone they touched. Over a hundred vacationers were fatally engulfed in the swirling fire. One hundred fifty more were scattered on the blackened sand, badly scorched. Those who leaped into the salt water to put out the flames on their bodies were tortured by

DEATH ON SALE! OVER 100 JAPANESE DIED WHEN A RAGING FIRE SWEPT THROUGH THE TAIYO DEPARTMENT STORE ON NOV. 30, 1973. THE SPRINKLER SYSTEM WASN'T IN OPERATION THAT DAY BECAUSE IT WAS BEING OVERHAULED *FOR FIRE PREVENTION WEEK!*

40 TONS OF T.N.T.!

STORED IN A LONDON MUNITIONS FACTORY BLEW SKY HIGH ON JANUARY 19, 1917-- IGNITED BY A SINGLE SPARK FROM THE CHIMNEY OF A NEARBY BUNGALOW!

THE REAL-LIFE TOWERING INFERNO!

FIREMEN IN SAO PAULO, BRAZIL, IN 1974 WATCHED HELPLESSLY AS **177** OFFICE WORKERS PERISHED IN A BLAZING 25-STORY SKYSCRAPER. THE BUILDING HAD NO FIRE ESCAPES, AND THE FIRE DEPARTMENT'S RESCUE LADDERS WERE TOO SHORT TO SAVE THOSE WHO ULTIMATELY LEAPT *TO THEIR DEATHS FROM OPEN WINDOWS!*

a ghastly chemical reaction that made the burning even worse. According to a French survivor, "It was like napalm, it was an inferno."

There were just too many guests at the June wedding in Lahore, Pakistan. The house suddenly crumbled under their weight, and thirty of the celebrants were found crushed in the wreckage.

The Great Chicago Fire

Although many of the city's firemen were still exhausted from fighting a disastrous blaze the day before, when another alarm came in on the night of October 8, 1871, they hauled out the wagons again and raced to Mrs. O'Leary's barn in the West Division of Chicago. They had no idea then that they were to be only a few minutes too late to avert at that time the worst conflagration to befall an American city.

Legend has it that Mrs. O'Leary's cow started the blaze by kicking over a kerosene lamp, but no one will ever know for sure what caused the fire. By the time the firemen arrived on the scene, not only the barn was ablaze, but several adjoining houses had been ignited by the flying sparks. The summer and fall of '71 had been extremely dry, and the preponderance of wooden structures in Chicago were ready kindling. The firefighters worked bravely, but in vain, to stop the spreading flames. Soon a whole city block had been razed.

The treacherous wind blew the fire relentlessly through the city forcing thousands from their homes as the wall of flame bore down the streets, consuming everything in its path. Many of the 100,000 Chicagoans made suddenly homeless by the fire took refuge in the chill waters of Lake Michigan, inching farther from shore as the pall of smoke grew denser and the hot cinders dropped from the sky. Firemen from neighboring cities and states rushed to the stricken city to help in the battle. But it wasn't until after midnight on October 10, two days after the blaze began, that the terrible destruction came to an end. Over 17,000 buildings had been burned to the ground, and property damage was estimated at $400,000,000; almost 70 insurance companies went bankrupt as a result. Three hundred lives had been lost in the deadly inferno and 200 more people were listed as missing.

Many of the dispirited survivors predicted the city would never to able to reclaim its place as one of America's most prosperous cities, but—as we know today—they were wrong. Within one year, half of Chicago had been rebuilt. And within one decade, hardly a trace of the Great Fire was left to be seen.

The Consolidated School in New London, Texas, was something the local citizens could point to with justifiable pride. Built at an estimated cost of one million dollars, it was probably the biggest "country" school in America in 1937, offering instruction to fifteen hundred students from a thirty-square-mile area.

But despite its recent construction, the school had been built with a fatal flaw. For economic reasons, natural gas was used to heat the building. An unsuspected leak in the pipes allowed the gas to accumulate in the tile walls, and on a Thursday

HEROIC RESCUE
OF WORLD'S MOST FAMOUS MIDGETS!
FIRE RAVAGED A MILWAUKEE HOTEL IN 1883! THROUGH FLAME AND SMOKE COURAGEOUS FIREMAN VAN HAAG *SAVED THE LIVES OF GEN. TOM THUMB AND HIS WIFE BY CARRYING THEM, ONE UNDER EACH ARM, TO A FIRE ESCAPE!*

afternoon in March, just fifteen minutes before classes would be dismissed for the day, something, perhaps a faulty light switch, ignited the pent-up gas. Instantly, there was an explosion so violent that the school's massive roof was lifted into the air. The walls crumbled; cinder blocks flew. And then the catastrophe was over. As the dust slowly settled over the mountain of rubble and the shattered bodies of over four hundred pupils, the showplace school of Texas was now its most tragic ruin.

The Burning of Rome

In 64 A.D., Rome was a sprawling metropolis. The rich and powerful citizens of the city lived in beautiful villas in quiet residential districts, while the teeming multitudes were crowded into an endless maze of dark, dirty streets, in rickety buildings. The thickly-congested city was ripe for disaster. And it struck.

For some weeks, there had been no rain; the air was hot and dry. The streets of the city were virtually deserted when the first tongues of flame began to lick at the flammable goods stored in the shops and taverns of the business district. A strong wind sprang up and carried the flames beyond the burning shops and warehouses, into the surrounding streets. The fire spread rapidly—so rapidly that the people were unable to contain it as they had similar blazes in the past. Rumors flew that the fire had intentionally been set by enemies of Rome, that a squad of secret arsonists was igniting each district in turn.

NOW, THAT'S SENSURROUND!

MOVIEGOERS IN PORT CHICAGO, CA., WERE WATCHING A BOMBING SCENE IN A WAR FILM WHEN A MUNITIONS SHIP NEARBY EXPLODED, **BLOWING IN ONE WALL OF THE THEATER!**

Messengers dispatched with news of the fire to the Emperor's villa at Anzio made little impression at first. Nero and his court believed the conflagration posed no threat to the city and that it would soon be put out. But as these messengers were succeeded by others, each bearing more alarming news of the widespread destruction, it became clear that the hub of the Empire was, after all, in danger of total ruin. Nero called for his horse.

When he arrived after a hard ride to the smoke-filled capital, he immediately set to work organizing shelters and finding food supplies for the distraught populace. But his presence, he found, provided little encouragement or comfort to the people. Many believed that Nero had ordered the fire set and the legend has persisted that he did so in order to compose a poem and play his lyre to the vaulting flames.

For six days and seven nights the fire raged, climbing as high as the statue of Jupiter on the Capitol. Gone were the Vestals Temple, the great altar dedicated to Hercules, the palace of King Huma, the treasures of Greek and Roman art. Ten of Rome's fourteen districts were reduced to blackened rubble, and hundreds of thousands of people were without food or shelter. Neighboring cities sent much-needed supplies, huts were hastily constructed in the Emperor's Gardens, and the huge task of raising a new and more beautiful Rome from the still smoldering ashes was begun.

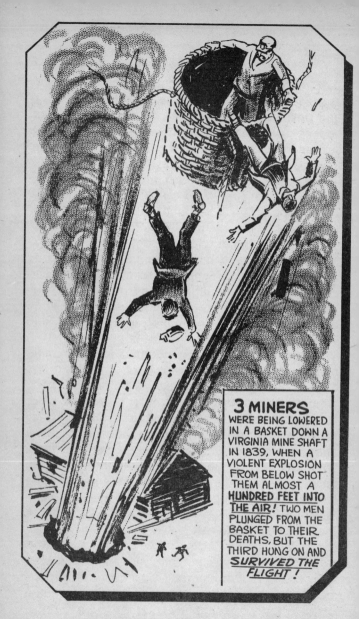

3 MINERS WERE BEING LOWERED IN A BASKET DOWN A VIRGINIA MINE SHAFT IN 1839, WHEN A VIOLENT EXPLOSION FROM BELOW SHOT THEM ALMOST A **HUNDRED FEET INTO THE AIR!** TWO MEN PLUNGED FROM THE BASKET TO THEIR DEATHS, BUT THE THIRD HUNG ON AND *SURVIVED THE FLIGHT!*

Chemical Reaction!

Someone made a mistake in mixing chemicals at the O'Connor Electroplating Company in Los Angeles, California on February 20, 1947. The fatal error resulted in a massive explosion that leveled the plant and four nearby blocks of buildings! Fifteen people died in the blast and another 158 were injured.

Close Encounters

If there are no known fatalities from meteors crashing to earth, that is largely a matter of luck.

In 1847, a meteorite plunged through the roof of a house in the Bohemian region of Czechoslovakia, narrowly missing three terrified children.

In 1947, a meteor plummeted to earth in Siberia, pulverizing rocks in the area and throwing uprooted trees miles into the sky!

But it was in 1908 that the great Siberian meteor fell from the sky. A Russian farmer fifty miles away from where it landed watched it streak across the heavens, and said he could feel its incredible heat. When it crashed into a forest swamp, the blast was heard for hundreds of miles. Great clouds of dust and smoke billowed into the sky and created stunning sunsets over Europe for days afterwards. A peasant living miles away lost many of his reindeer herd from the percussion.

When scientists visited the site twenty years later, they found that the tundra forest had been utterly destroyed for an area of one thousand square

WITCHES' REVENGE?

ON JUNE 25, 1914 FIRE SPREAD OVER 3 SQ. MILES OF THE OLD SEAPORT TOWN OF SALEM, MASS. THOUGH OVER 1,000 BUILDINGS WERE DESTROYED AND 10,000 PEOPLE MADE HOMELESS, THE **WITCHES' HOUSE** ···WHERE CONDEMNED WITCHES WERE KEPT FOR EXECUTION··· *WAS THE ONLY HISTORIC LANDMARK TO BE COMPLETELY DESTROYED!*

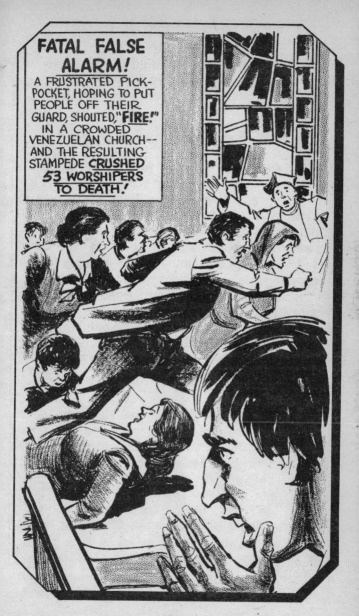

FATAL FALSE ALARM!
A FRUSTRATED PICK-POCKET, HOPING TO PUT PEOPLE OFF THEIR GUARD, SHOUTED, "**FIRE!**" IN A CROWDED VENEZUELAN CHURCH-- AND THE RESULTING STAMPEDE **CRUSHED** *53* WORSHIPERS TO DEATH!

miles! The meteor itself, thought to be a piece of the Pons-Winnecke comet, had burrowed so deeply into the earth that it has never been discovered.

The Bridge That Failed

It began with a publicity stunt for a traveling circus. Handbills announced to the inhabitants of Yarmouth, England, that a clown would be pulled up the river in a boat drawn by four fat geese. At the appointed time, hundreds of people, chiefly mothers and their children, were gathered on the town's suspension bridge to enjoy the novel sight. Suddenly someone shouted "Here come the geese!" and a moment later, the overloaded bridge collapsed, plunging the huge crowd into the fast-moving river below. Fishermen along the banks jumped into their boats and rowed to the rescue, but they were too late to save the lives of 250 of the unfortunate spectators.

The Iroquois Theater Disaster

On June 4, 1978, a lighted match fell on a carpet in Chicago's Oriental Theater. Moments later, flames were creeping down the lavishly decorated corridor and clouds of smoke began to fill the house. But the two thousand movie-goers inside were safely evacuated and the theater itself was saved from destruction—all because of an earlier fire, a fire that had claimed over six hundred lives, on that very spot, seventy-five years before!

Where the Oriental Theater stands today, there

362 BODIES WERE RECOVERED AFTER A TRAGIC EXPLOSION IN A MONONGAH, W. VIRGINIA COAL MINE-- *BUT ONE OF THEM WASN'T A MINER!* HE WAS A LOCAL BUSINESSMAN WHO HAD BEEN DOWN IN THE TUNNELS TRYING TO SELL LIFE INSURANCE!

TEARS OF A CLOWN!

THE SAD FACE OF CIRCUS CLOWN EMMETT KELLY WAS TRAGICALLY APPROPRIATE ON JULY 6, 1944, WHEN *THE BIG TOP BURST INTO FLAMES!* THOUGH KELLY AND OTHER PERFORMERS COURAGEOUSLY GUIDED MANY TO SAFETY, <u>168 PEOPLE DIED IN THE CONFLAGRATION!</u>

once was a beautiful auditorium called The Iroquois. It was billed as "fireproof." But during an afternoon performance on December 30, 1903, the draperies backstage were suddenly set ablaze by an open arc light. A stagehand frantically tried to put it out with a fire extinguisher, but the flames raced up to the ceiling and swept across the stage. The asbestos curtain, designed to protect the audience in just such an emergency, started to drop, and then jammed.

The star of the show, Eddie Foy, ran onto the stage and tried to calm the panic-stricken crowd. He shouted at the orchestra to keep on playing, but someone opened a backstage door and the draft blew a huge wall of fire into the auditorium. The mob surged toward the exit doors, but many of them were locked, and others, built to open inwards, were useless because of the terrified people crushing against them.

Before firemen could extinguish the blaze, 575 people had perished inside. Twenty-seven others would die of their injuries later. But as a result of the awful catastrophe, strict theater-safety laws would be instituted. Automatic sprinklers, fire-resistant curtains, emergency lighting systems, and many other precautions would all become mandatory. And over the years, these safety measures would pay off time and again.

7

Disease
and Pestilence

The Black Death

Of the countless disasters to befall mankind, the worst by far was the pandemic of bubonic plague that swept across the face of Europe during the Middle Ages. Anywhere from one-third to one-half of the total population perished from the dread desease, and the course of world history was seriously altered.

The infection was caused by a lethal bacillus that was harbored by fleas, and which the fleas then transmitted to rats, other animals, or humans. The bubonic plague attacked the lymph system, bursting blood vessels and producing dark splotches all over the victim's skin. Because it caused the tongue to turn black, the plague came to be known as the Black Death.

It arrived in Europe in October 1347 on board a fleet of Genoese ships. The sailors had become infected at one of their ports-of-call in the eastern Mediterranean, and by the time they sailed into the Sicilian harbor of Messina, they were highly contagious. The harbor authorities ordered the ships away immediately, but they were already too late. Terrified residents, already infected, abandoned the city and carried the disease throughout Italy and into France. By August of the following year it had reached England.

It is almost impossible to imagine the full extent of the horror. Whole towns were desolated. People crazed with fear abandoned their families, their religion, and all hope. Those who could be pressed into service carted the dead out of the ravaged cities and dumped their swollen bodies into huge common graves. The carcasses of thousands of infected animals lay rotting in the countryside. On the seas, ships drifted aimlessly with the wind and the current, all of the sailors dead.

Eventually, the Black Death subsided, but it did not disappear. It resurfaced in Europe in 1361, and again in the Great Plague of London in 1665. Even today, according to studies made by the World Health Organization of the United Nations, the Black Death exists in a dormant state.

Yellow Fever Epidemic

The first symptoms of the disease were chills and a suffusion of blood in the face. Within two days, the skin of the victim had become so hot the physician couldn't touch it without being hurt. To ward off the disease, people swallowed vinegar and disinfected anything they came in contact with. When walking outside, they held to their faces sponges doused with camphor and always tried to stay on the windward side of anyone with whom they stopped to chat. But even with all these precautions, many lives were lost to the epidemic of yellow fever that raged through the eastern United States in 1895. In New York alone, over 700 people died, their bodies carted off to the charnel house at Bellevue Hospital.

DANCE of DEATH!

VICTIMS OF A DEADLY EPIDEMIC IN 15th CENTURY ITALY OFTEN WHIRLED ABOUT WILDLY IN THEIR PAIN. ONLOOKERS THOUGHT THEY'D BEEN **STUNG BY TARANTULAS** AND NAMED THE FAMOUS FOLK DANCE THAT CHARACTERIZED THEIR AGONIES THE **TARANTELLA!**

THE **ONLY REFUGE** ...

AN INVISIBLE KILLER, THE **SPANISH INFLUENZA** OF 1918, **KILLED OVER 21 MILLION PEOPLE, IN EVERY REGION OF THE WORLD EXCEPT ONE** -- THE LITTLE SO. AMERICAN ISLAND OF **TRISTAN DA CUNHA**!

Tristan da Cunha

The dreaded yellow fever has even played a part in world history. During the attempt to build the Panama Canal so many French workers fell ill the project was given up as hopeless. And when Teddy Roosevelt's Rough Riders returned to America from the Spanish-American War, many of them carried the fever inside them. Hospitals were quickly set up at the debarkation point, but for many of the soldiers afflicted with the disease the ward would be their last sight of America.

Itching Epidemic

During the Middle Ages, a strange and horrible disease afflicted many people in France and Germany. It was called St. Anthony's Fire, and it caused the hands and feet of its victims to itch painfully and burn. Soon the fingers and toes actually fell off, and the disease then moved up the arms and legs.

For well over five hundred years, the dreaded disease caused by moldy rye grain continued to sporadically erupt in Europe.

An American Plague

During the colonial era, the eastern seaboard of this country was swept by deadly epidemics of smallpox. They seemed to erupt every five years, and the cities from Boston to New Orleans lived in dread of the next outbreak. The worst came in 1731, when the disease took 500 lives in New York. At that time, the city had only nine thousand citizens. In Boston, Cotton Mather advised his friends to have their slaves inoculated with a primitive remedy called Lady Mary Wortley Montagu's vaccine. This cure, unfortunately, was nearly as awful as the disease inself.

Napoleon Bonaparte struggled to save his army from the dread embrace of the Black Plague. During his Syrian campaign, many of his soldiers fell

A STRANGE DISEASE CALLED THE **ENGLISH SWEATS** KILLED THOUSANDS OF ENGLISH CITIZENS IN 1485-- BUT **ONLY IN THE UPPER CLASSES!**

DEADLY WEDDING !

OVER **100** REVELERS AT A NEW DELHI WEDDING FEAST IN 1972 WERE **FATALLY POISONED BY BOOTLEG LIQUOR,** BUT THE POLICE COULD NOT ARREST THE BOOTLEGGER-- **HE HAD ALREADY DIED** AS HE WAS ONE OF THE WEDDING GUESTS **WHO DRANK THE LETHAL LIQUOR !**

A **MAN-EATING TIGRESS** TERRORIZED THE CHAMPAWAT DISTRICT OF INDIA IN 1907, SLAUGHTERING **436 NATIVES** BEFORE BEING SHOT BY AN ARMY OFFICER NAMED JIM CORBETT!

260 SURVIVORS

OF A PORTUGUESE STEAMER SHIPWRECKED OFF AFRICA REPORTEDLY SWAM THROUGH SHARK-INFESTED WATERS -- *ONLY TO FIND A HORDE OF HUNGRY LIONS PROWLING THE BEACH !*

gravely ill and in order to bolster their spirits, he visited the plague hospital at Jaffa and touched the victims' sores. "You see, it is nothing," he said.

The army doctor was equally courageous. While his patients looked on, he gave himself an inoculation of the plague and followed the same treatment procedures he advocated for them.

The Winged Famine

'And the locusts went up over all the land of Egypt, and rested in all the coasts of Egypt; very grievous were they. . . . For they covered the face of the whole earth, so that the land was darkened; and they did eat every herb of the land, and all the fruit of the trees which the hail had left; and there remained not any green thing in the trees, or in the herbs of the field, through all the land of Egypt'.

That is how the Bible grimly and accurately describes the terrible devastation left in the wake of a plague of locusts. Throughout time, these insect swarms, sometimes measuring as much as twenty miles in depth and cumulatively weighing thousands of tons, have caused widespread destruction and famine. St. Augustine wrote of a locust horde that descended upon North Africa, devouring everything edible for miles around. Eight hundred thousand people died in the resulting famine. And in 591, almost a million people and cattle died after a swarm of locusts swept across Italy. Most of the victims died of starvation, but many others were killed by a fever generated by the mounting piles of dead, decomposing insects.

144

CULT OF DEATH!

SHORTLY AFTER THE FATEFUL DAY OF NOV. 18, 1978, THE PEOPLES TEMPLE WOULD BE A RELIGIOUS CULT KNOWN TO ALL! WHILE UNDER THE MANIACAL LEADERSHIP OF REVEREND JIM JONES, OVER **900 PEOPLE**, INCLUDING **260 CHILDREN**, DRANK A LETHAL DOSE OF CYANIDE IN **A COMBINATION SUICIDE AND MASS-MURDER** THAT SHOCKED AND HORRIFIED AN UNSUSPECTING WORLD!

Slaughter in Guyana

Inside the Reverend Jim Jones there seemed to live both a saint and a demon. A devout Christian since his boyhood in Indiana, Jones had often displayed a generous and altruistic nature—adopting eight children, running neighborhood churches that distributed free food and clothing, helping his destitute parishioners to locate jobs. But alongside his humanitarian zeal, there had always been a strangely sinister and unbalanced streak.

It was in the newly established community of Jonestown in the jungles of Guyana that the demon of Reverend Jones truly gained the upper hand. He, with over nine hundred members of his church which he called the People's Temple, purchased 27,000 acres of land in the small South American country. Blackmail, fear and violence were the tools Jones used to ensure obedience. Public whippings were held to instill fear. On what were called "white nights," all the Jonestown colonists were roused from sleep and instructed to drink a liquid that they were told was poison. After passing this "loyalty test," Jones' followers were assured the drink was harmless—but reminded that someday it might not be.

That day came on November 18, 1978. Leo Ryan, a California Congressman, had heard rumors of the grim way in which Jones ran his colony and had flown there to see for himself. After his inspection tour, fourteen of the colonists asked to leave with Ryan and his party. Jones appeared to acquiesce. While the congressman and his party were preparing to depart at the airstrip, a tractor-trailer appeared with three armed men on it. They opened fire, killing Ryan, three newsmen and one of the Jonestown defectors. The others in Ryan's party managed to escape, and Jones' soldiers returned to the settlement.

All the colonists were assembled by Jones in the main pavilion. Surrounded by guards armed with guns or bows and arrows, they were exhorted to drink a fatal concoction of a fruit drink laced with cyanide. Jones warned that any survivor would be tortured by Guyanese army soldiers. A few people were able to escape into the jungle, but some *nine hundred* of the Jonestown men, women and children, willingly or unwillingly, drank the lethal liquid and died within five minutes. The Reverend Jones reportedly died soon after from a self-imposed gunshot wound.

This will surely be remembered as one of history's most appalling instances of mass suicide and murder. The saint in the Reverend Jim Jones had perished long ago; now the demon was at last dead, too.

Transportation
Disasters

The "Unsinkable" *TITANIC*

It was a clear and windless night in the spring of 1912, and one of the world's largest ships, the *Titanic,* was steaming toward New York on her maiden voyage. The pride of the British White Star Line, the *Titanic* boasted a watertight design and had been advertised as positively "unsinkable."

The months preceding its launching had been unusually warm, and a flock of giant icebergs had splintered off the polar icecaps and drifted into the North Atlantic. One of these deadly monsters was on a collision course with the unsuspecting *Titanic.*

The first to see its icy bulk looming up fifty feet above the dark water was the lookout on the *Titanic*'s crow's nest. He rang out a loud warning on the ship's bell, then shouted into the phone to the bridge, "Iceberg, right ahead!"

The ship lunged hard to starboard, then to port, trying to avert a collision, but the iceberg hit, slicing through two boiler rooms and three of the underwater holds. The freezing waters of the North Atlantic rushed into the ship through a gaping hole three hundred feet long!

The *Titanic* came to a dead halt. The captain ordered all hands on deck and stewards calmly instructed the passengers to leave their cabins, ominously adding that they should bring their life preservers with them.

The wireless operator frantically tapped out the new code distress signal: "SOS, SOS, SOS, *Titanic* sinking hard by the bow . . ." It was the first SOS ever dispatched.

Only five miles away, the Captain of the *Californian* observed the emergency red and white flares the *Titanic* sent rocketing into the night sky. Mistaking them for party fireworks he went below for a good night's sleep.

Two ships, however, received the wireless signal and raced toward the sinking *Titanic*. One was her sister ship, the *Olympic*, five hundred miles away, and the other a rusty Cunard liner named the *Carpathia*. But neither would arrive in time to avert the tragic loss of life.

As the bow of the *Titanic* slowly dipped deeper into the ocean, the lifeboats—far too few to accommodate all the passengers—were loaded with women and children and lowered into the sea. Approximately 1500 doomed passengers and crewmen watched helplessly as the last boat pulled away. The ship's band bravely remained on deck, playing "Londonderry Air" and the hymn "Autumn."

Suddenly, with a mighty blast that tore through the interior of the crippled ship the boilers exploded. The stern rose high into the air and with a thundering roar the ship slipped quickly under the water. An hour later, the creaking old *Carpathia* arrived to rescue the 711 survivors of the "unsinkable" *Titanic*'s first—and last—voyage.

THE CURSE THAT SANK THE TITANIC!

ACCORDING TO SOME REPORTS, THE MIGHTY OCEAN LINER **TITANIC** WAS SUNK BY THE **"BLACK BUDDAH,"** A PRICELESS STATUE CONCEALED IN THE CAPTAIN'S SAFE. STUDDED *WITH MILLIONS OF DOLLARS WORTH OF GEMS, THE BUDDAH CARRIED WITH IT A DEADLY CURSE!*

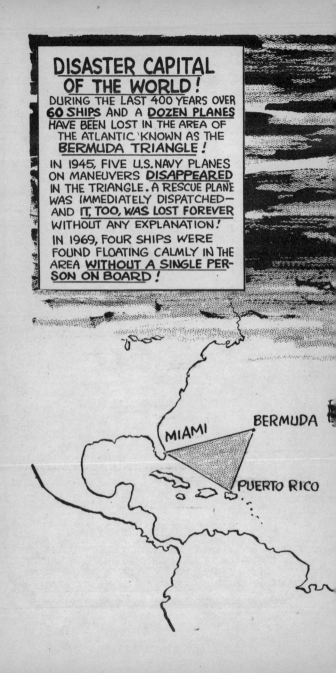

Tunnel of Death

In the early morning hours of March 2, 1944, two straining engines pulled forty-seven train cars out of the little Italian town of Balvano. Aboard the long train were hundreds of passengers who had simply jumped aboard once the train had crawled out of the station. No sooner had the overloaded train entered the Mount Armi tunnel, built on a steep incline, than it began to slow down and stall, either as a result of burning low-grade coal that provided too little heat for the engines, or simply because of the excessive number of people on board. The two engineers couldn't decide whether to build up a bigger head of steam and try to make it through the tunnel, or to let the train slide backwards down the hill. While they debated the alternatives, the tunnel rapidly filled with clouds of black smoke, containing a lethal carbon monoxide level. In a matter of seconds, the engineers were dead at the controls. The billowing smoke blew back through the train cars, choking the passengers trapped helplessly inside. Only those in the last few cars, which had stopped short of the tunnel entrance, survived the ghastly accident. A brakeman ran down the line for help and returned with rescuers. But they were too late to revive any of the 509 passengers who had suffocated in the black tunnel of Mount Armi.

The Storm That Saved Greece

Xerxes the Great, King of Persia in the 5th century B.C., was preparing to invade Greece. He had as-

COLLISION COURSE!

IN THE SKIES OVER STATEN ISLAND, N.Y., ON DEC. 16, 1960, A TWA SUPER CONSTELLATION AND A UNITED DC-8 JET <u>COLLIDED KILLING ALL ABOARD</u>!

THE CRIPPLED DC-8 CRASHED TO EARTH IN BROOKLYN, WHERE IT BURIED ITSELF <u>IN FLAMES IN THE PILLAR OF FIRE CHURCH</u>!

ONLY FOUR YEARS BEFORE, THE <u>SAME</u> TWO AIRLINES HAD BEEN INVOLVED IN A COLLISION OVER THE GRAND CANYON AND LOST <u>THE SAME NUMBER OF PASSENGERS AND CREW</u>!

"DEAD MAN'S CONTROLS"
(AUTOMATIC BRAKES) WERE INSTALLED IN ALL NEW JERSEY PASSENGER TRAINS AFTER THE BAYONNE DISASTER OF 1958, WHEN A COMMUTER TRAIN RACED THROUGH AN OPEN DRAWBRIDGE DROWNING 48 IN NEWARK BAY! IT WAS THOUGHT THAT AT THE MOMENT THE TRAIN REACHED THE WARNING LIGHTS *BOTH THE ENGINEER AND FIRE-MAN SUFFERED SIMULTANEOUS HEART ATTACKS!*

TWO-TIME LOSER! IN 1964 THE AUSTRALIAN AIRCRAFT CARRIER MELBOURNE COLLIDED WITH ONE OF ITS OWN DESTROYERS, THE VOYAGER. NO SOONER HAD IT BEEN REFITTED FOR SERVICE, AT A COST OF NEARLY $8,000,000, THAN IT SMASHED INTO A U.S. BATTLESHIP DURING SEATO MANEUVERS!

sembled hundreds of ships and thousands of soldiers to ensure himself of triumph. But on the dawn of the day set for the attack, a terrible storm blew out of the east and tore into the Persian armada. Over 400 ships were sent to the bottom of the ocean, with numberless soldiers aboard. What survived of the once invincible Persian fleet sailed for home, vanquished, not by an enemy, but by the violent wind and sea.

Independence Day Disaster

The streetcar in Tacoma, Washington, was packed with people celebrating the Fourth of July, 1900. Suddenly the overloaded trolley, descending a steep hill, went out of control and plunged downwards. Terrified passengers leaped from the platforms and mothers caught inside threw their children out the windows of the racing car. Moments later, the trolley flipped into the air and landed on its roof, the heavy wheels tearing through the floor. Forty-one riders were killed in the wreck.

Six passengers in an aerial cablecar fell to their deaths in the icy Vallée Blanche when a low-flying French army jet accidentally cut through the suspension cable!

Worst Air Disaster Ever!

On March 27, 1977, a swirling fog shrouded the Los Rodeos Airport in the Canary Islands. A massive Pan Am 747 was taxiing off the main runway when

BIRD VERSUS JET!
THE FIRST AMERICAN ASTRONAUT TO LOSE HIS LIFE
WAS CAPTAIN THEODORE C. FREEMAN, KILLED WHEN A
*GOOSE STRUCK THE WINDSHIELD
OF HIS T-38 JET TRAINER!*

a KLM 747 suddenly appeared through the mist, approaching at take-off speed! The KLM pilot frantically tried to raise his craft off the ground while the Pan Am plane swerved to the left, but it was already too late! The Dutch plane tore the roof off part of the Pan Am jet, then exploded in the air in a ball of fire! The 248 passengers and crewmen on board were instantly killed. Only moments later, the mutilated Pan Am plane also exploded, throwing its burning wreckage all over the airfield. Three hundred thirty-two of its passengers died in the blast and the ensuing fire.

After lengthy investigations into the collision, authorities had to conclude that this most murderous disaster in aviation history had been simply the result of a misunderstood or unheard instruction from the control tower to the pilot of the KLM jet.

Golden Cargo

When the United States ship *Golden Gate* steamed out of San Francisco harbor in July 1862 it carried a very fitting cargo—one-and-a-half-million dollars in gold and silver, including a chest filled with $50 octagonal-shaped gold pieces.

But the precious cargo never reached its destination. Off the coast of Mexico, the ship burned and went to the bottom, with 175 people aboard. Ever since, treasure hunters have been lured to the wreck, including Duncan Johnston who, in 1900, was able to salvage $500,000 in gold!

AGAINST ALL ODDS!

LOST IN A FOG IN 1945, A U.S. B-25 BOMBER CRASHED INTO THE 79th FLOOR OF THE EMPIRE STATE BUILDING, KILLING 14 PEOPLE. THE ODDS AGAINST JUST SUCH AN ACCIDENT HAVE BEEN COMPUTED AT 10,000 TO 1!

WHITE DEATH!

IN THE WORST AVALANCHE IN U.S. HISTORY, A WALL OF SNOW THREW SEVERAL TRAINS--AND THE TRAIN STATION, TOO-- INTO A CANYON 150 FEET DEEP! OVER A HUNDRED PEOPLE WERE KILLED IN THE FALL!

Cascade Mt., Wash.
-1910-

TRAPPED BELOW DECKS ON THE BURNING SHIP _SAALE_, PASSENGERS AND CREW RECEIVED <u>FINAL ABSOLUTION</u> FROM FATHER JOHN BROSNAN, WHO ADMINISTERED THE BLESSING <u>THROUGH</u> THE <u>ELEVEN-INCH PORTHOLES!</u>

The Birkenhead Heroes

The naval traditions of "women and children first" and "going down with the ship" seem to have been around forever, but they actually were established in 1852 by the soldiers and sailors aboard the British steamer *Birkenhead*.

The ship was loaded with troops on their way to South Africa to fight the Kaffirs. Also on board were some of the officers' wives and children. In the dead of night, the ship ran aground on treacherous rocks off the Cape of Good Hope, and before they could even be awakened many of the soldiers in the forward hold were drowned. The ship's captain was able to extricate the ship from the rocks, but the damage was too great to keep it from sinking. The men were ordered on deck and commanded to stand in orderly ranks while the only three lifeboats that could be launched were filled with the women and children. Their ranks never broke as the ship was evacuated and began to disintegrate around them. Over 400 of the *Birkenhead*'s soldiers went down with the ship that fateful February night. Their heroism was immortalized by Rudyard Kipling in a famous poem entitled "The Birken'ead Drill."

Tragic Excursion

It was meant to be a special treat for the ladies, a one-day shopping excursion for women who had, for the most part, never been far from the small British towns in which they lived. But it ended in

NELLIE O'DONNELL HAD NEVER LEARNED TO SWIM ··· BUT WHEN SHE SAW AN EXCURSION BOAT, THE "GEN. SLOCUM," SINKING IN NEW YORK'S EAST RIVER, WITH HUNDREDS OF WOMEN AND CHILDREN DROWNING, SHE JUMPED INTO THE WATER AND SAVED TEN LIVES BEFORE COLLAPSING WITH EXHAUSTION!

TELEPHONE CALL TO A DEAD MAN!
WHEN THE NAVY DIRIGIBLE <u>AKRON</u> PLUNGED INTO THE
ATLANTIC WITH <u>SEVENTY-SIX CREW MEMBERS ABOARD</u>,
NAVY OFFICIALS QUICKLY CALLED REAR ADMIRAL MOFFET,
LEADING BLIMP ADVOCATE, TO NOTIFY HIM OF THE
TRAGEDY. WHEN HIS WIFE ANSWERED THE PHONE AND
WAS GIVEN THE AWFUL MESSAGE, SHE NUMBLY REPLIED
THAT HER HUSBAND HAD BEEN ABOARD!

DEATH
AT 180 M.P.H.

OUT OF CONTROL, A MERCEDES BENZ SLASHED INTO THE CROWD AND EXPLODED AT THE 1955 LE MANS AUTO RACE ⋯ THOUGH 77 SPECTATORS WERE TORN TO PIECES, OFFICIALS INSISTED THAT *THE RACE GO ON!*

tragedy when the chartered plane on its way to Switzerland flew into thick fog and swirling snow. On its second attempt to complete an instrument landing outside of Basel, the plane crashed to earth and then exploded! Over a hundred of the women aboard, most of them mothers, perished in the wreck.

Even the elaborate computer controls couldn't avert the catastrophe in Mexico City's subway system. Somebody pulled an emergency cord on a morning train, and moments later a second commuter train smashed into it from behind! Rescue workers had to dismantle part of the subway station roof in order to extricate some of the twenty-six dead and 170 injured.

A DC-3 jetliner on a training flight over Lovettsville, Virginia, crashed after its crew had been temporarily blinded by a flash of lightning! This is the only U.S. airliner on record which crashed because of lightning!

A Second Titanic

The builders of the *Hans Hedtoft,* just like the builders of the ill-fated *Titanic*, believed their ship was virtually unsinkable. She was specially designed for traveling in northern waters, with seven watertight compartments and steel armor on both her bow and stern. In addition to all the most modern navigation equipment, including radar, the *Hans Hed-*

toft's master was a veteran captain used to sailing in Polar waters.

But it was on the return leg of her maiden voyage, while passing just south of Greenland, that the ship was caught in rough seas, and suddenly collided with a massive iceberg! She immediately radioed for help, and though a German trawler arrived on the scene only an hour after the last signal had been sent, not a trace of the "unsinkable" *Hans Hedtoft*—or its ninety-five passengers and crewmen—was ever found.

PRIDE OF THE
NAZI AIR FORCE!
THE ZEPPELIN HINDENBURG
IS THOUGHT TO HAVE EXPLODED
AFTER A SABOTEUR IMPLANTED
IN ITS HYDROGEN CELLS
A *SIMPLE PHOTOGRAPHER'S
FLASHBULB!*